just for
two

THE AUSTRALIAN
Women's Weekly

contents

Cooking for two is a lovely way to prepare food: twice the fun with half the effort. You can experiment, you can use "grown-up" ingredients, you don't have to spend a lot of time readying huge quantities or waiting hours for them to cook, you don't have to cater for a raft of different palates... it's almost as good as cooking for just yourself! Plus, you'll find it's very easy to eat healthier when you only cook for two, simpler and fresher. Enjoy – and re-discover how much fun cooking can be.

Pamela Clark

Food Director

tips for two

Whether DINKs, empty-nesters, or any of the other two-adult households that comprise such a large percentage of today's urban populations, most of us truly enjoy cooking real food, good food, for pleasure as much as for sustenance. Cooking for just the two of you rekindles interest after years of catering for children, provides comfort from the stresses of the outside world and releases untapped levels of creativity. And isn't it nice to know that there's that extra bit of disposable income to spend on premium produce and upscale ingredients? It's much more fun to cook when you aren't concerned about having to "make-do". Shopping and cooking for two means you can buy what you really like, when you really want it, and splurge on experimental or expensive items since the quantity is smaller. Here, we've given you a great selection of reliable, effortless main course and divine dessert recipes downsized just right for two.

- When you buy a large cut of meat, cut and wrap it into two-person portions, then label then freeze them. These smaller pieces of meat thaw much faster than larger quantities.
- It's a good idea to buy smaller portions of more kinds of vegetables and fruit; you won't have to throw out spoiled leftovers and, by choosing exactly the amount you need, you can experiment with new varieties you're not familiar with without worrying about wasting money. Treat yourself to rare and exotic fruits and vegetables; try using fresh herbs you've never used before.
- Make mealtime special: spend extra time on presentation; think about how food is plated in a restaurant; use garnishes.
- Most bottles and jars can be covered and stored in the refrigerator if you don't use all of their contents. Repackage food that comes in cans or plastic containers into glass.
- Smaller appliances such as a toaster oven or a mini food processor are adequate for cooking two-person quantities, and are easier to clean, more energy-efficient and take up less kitchen space.
- Think about turning leftovers into the basis of a small casserole or, conversely, cook larger casseroles and then divide the leftovers into two-person portions and freeze. Cooking larger quantities of food and using the leftovers in other recipes also reduces the amount of time spent in your kitchen.
- Browse the ethnic food aisle of your supermarket or make a visit to an Asian or Middle Eastern food shop and discover brand new worlds of flavours and ideas. Use various ethnic seasonings to add flair to some of your more basic recipes.
- Barbecue year round: there are hundreds of barbecue sauce, marinade and rub ideas, each of which will give a different look and taste to the same cut of meat, poultry, fish or seafood.

A TABLE FOR TWO

banana pancakes

preparation time 10 minutes cooking time 10 minutes

½ cup (75g) self-raising flour

1 tablespoon caster sugar

⅔ cup (160ml) buttermilk

1 egg white, beaten lightly

1 tablespoon maple syrup

10g butter, melted

1 medium banana (200g), sliced thinly

2 tablespoons maple syrup, extra

¼ cup (30g) roasted pecans, chopped coarsely

1 Sift flour into medium bowl, stir in sugar. Whisk in combined buttermilk, egg white, maple syrup and butter until batter is smooth. Stir in banana.

2 Heat oiled large frying pan; pour ¼ cup of the batter into pan. Cook, uncovered, until bubbles appear on surface. Turn pancake; cook until browned lightly. Remove from pan, cover to keep warm. Repeat with remaining batter.

3 Serve pancakes topped with extra maple syrup and sprinkled with nuts.
per serving 17.1g total fat (4.5g saturated fat); 2153kJ (515 cal); 78.5g carbohydrate; 11.4g protein; 4.1g fibre

BREAKFAST

baked eggs with pancetta

preparation time 10 minutes cooking time 20 minutes

1 teaspoon olive oil

½ small red capsicum (75g), chopped finely

3 slices pancetta (45g), chopped finely

50g mushrooms, chopped finely

2 green onions, chopped finely

2 tablespoons finely grated parmesan cheese

4 eggs

2 teaspoons coarsely chopped
fresh flat-leaf parsley

1   Preheat oven to 200°C/180°C fan-forced. Lightly oil two ¾-cup (180ml) ovenproof dishes.

2   Heat oil in small frying pan; cook capsicum and pancetta, stirring, until capsicum is just tender. Add mushroom and onion; cook, stirring, until onion just softens. Remove from heat; stir in half the cheese.

3   Divide capsicum mixture among dishes; break two eggs into each dish. Bake in oven, uncovered, 5 minutes. Sprinkle remaining cheese over eggs; bake further 5 minutes or until eggs are just set. Sprinkle with parsley just before serving.

per serving 18.2g total fat (6.1g saturated fat); 1091kJ (261 cal); 2.5g carbohydrate; 21.8g protein; 1.3g fibre

blueberry bircher muesli

preparation time 15 minutes (plus standing time)

1 cup (90g) rolled oats

½ cup (125ml) fresh orange juice

½ cup (140g) natural yogurt

2 tablespoons honey

¼ cup (60ml) soy milk

1 small green apple (130g), grated coarsely

100g fresh blueberries

¼ cup (25g) roasted walnuts, chopped coarsely

1   Combine oats, juice, yogurt, honey and milk in medium bowl; stand 30 minutes.

2   Stir in apple. Serve muesli topped with blueberries and nuts.

per serving 15.8g total fat (2.8g saturated fat); 2032kJ (486 cal); 71.6g carbohydrate; 11.8g protein; 6.1g fibre

potato rösti with poached eggs and tomato relish

preparation time 15 minutes cooking time 15 minutes

2 teaspoons olive oil

2 small egg tomatoes (120g), halved

2 medium sebago potatoes (400g), peeled, grated coarsely

½ teaspoon salt

40g butter

2 eggs

2 tablespoons tomato relish

1 Heat oil in small frying pan; cook tomato until browned and tender. Remove from heat; cover to keep warm.

2 Meanwhile, combine potato and salt in medium bowl; squeeze out excess liquid. Melt half the butter in medium frying pan. Spread potato over pan, flatten. Cook, uncovered, over medium heat until golden underneath; invert onto plate.

3 Melt remaining butter in same pan, carefully slide potato rösti back into pan, uncooked-side down. Cook, uncovered, until browned lightly.

4 Meanwhile, half-fill a large shallow frying pan with water; bring to a boil. Break one egg into a cup, then slide into pan; repeat with remaining egg. Allow water to return to a boil. Cover pan, turn off heat; stand about 4 minutes or until a light film of egg white sets over yolks. Remove eggs, one at a time, using slotted spoon; place spoon on absorbent-paper-lined saucer briefly to blot up any poaching liquid.

5 Cut rösti into wedges; serve topped with eggs, tomato and relish.
per serving 26.5g total fat (13.1g saturated fat); 1668kJ (399 cal); 26.8g carbohydrate; 11.7g protein; 3.8g fibre

BREAKFAST

10

spiced plums with yogurt

preparation time 10 minutes cooking time 10 minutes (plus cooling time)

2 cups (500ml) water

¼ cup (60ml) orange juice

2 tablespoons caster sugar

2cm strip orange rind

2 cloves

½ teaspoon mixed spice

½ cinnamon stick

4 blood plums (400g), unpeeled

200g yogurt

1 Place the water, juice, sugar, rind and spices in small frying pan; cook mixture, stirring, until sugar dissolves.

2 Add plums to pan; poach, uncovered, over low heat about 10 minutes or until just tender. Using slotted spoon, place plums in serving dishes (reserve 2 tablespoons of the poaching liquid). Cool plums 20 minutes.

3 Combine yogurt and reserved poaching liquid in small bowl; serve with plums.

per serving 3.6g total fat (2.2g saturated fat); 911kJ (218 cal); 36.7g carbohydrate; 5.9g protein; 3.8g fibre

bacon and asparagus frittata

preparation time 15 minutes cooking time 45 minutes

4 bacon rashers (280g), rind removed, sliced thickly

1 large red onion (300g), sliced thinly

170g asparagus, trimmed, halved lengthways

4 eggs

4 egg whites

1 cup (250ml) buttermilk

1 Preheat oven to 180°C/160°C fan-forced. Oil deep 19cm-square cake pan; line base and sides with baking paper.

2 Cook bacon, stirring, in small heated frying pan until crisp; drain on absorbent paper. Add onion to pan; cook, stirring, until soft. Layer bacon, onion and asparagus in prepared pan.

3 Whisk eggs, egg whites and buttermilk in medium jug; pour into pan. Bake, uncovered, in oven, uncovered, about 35 minutes or until frittata is set. Stand 10 minutes before cutting into squares.

per serving 23.2g total fat (8.5g saturated fat); 1927kJ (461 cal); 17.2g carbohydrate; 44.4g protein; 3.2g fibre

TIP Leftover frittata can be served warm or cold.

warm rice porridge with stewed rhubarb

preparation time 15 minutes cooking time 30 minutes

1 vanilla bean

2 cups (500ml) milk

2 tablespoons caster sugar

1 strip orange rind

½ cup (100g) arborio rice

1 egg yolk

STEWED RHUBARB

2 cups (220g) coarsely chopped rhubarb

¼ cup (55g) caster sugar

1 tablespoon orange juice

1 Split vanilla bean lengthways, scrape out seeds. Place milk, sugar, rind, vanilla bean and seeds in medium heavy-based saucepan; bring to a simmer over medium heat.

2 Add rice to milk mixture; cook, stirring occasionally, about 30 minutes or until rice is tender. Add egg yolk; stir well to combine. Remove from heat; stand 5 minutes. Discard rind and vanilla bean.

3 Meanwhile, make stewed rhubarb.

4 Spoon rice mixture into serving bowls; top with stewed rhubarb.
   STEWED RHUBARB Place rhubarb, sugar and juice in medium, heavy-based saucepan over low heat; cook, stirring, about 15 minutes or until tender.
   per serving 13.1g total fat (7.3g saturated fat); 2408kJ (576 cal); 98.9g carbohydrate; 5.1g protein; 4g fibre

fetta and mint omelettes with crisp bacon

preparation time 10 minutes cooking time 20 minutes

4 bacon rashers (280g)

6 eggs

2 tablespoons water

40g butter

2 green onions, chopped finely

2 tablespoons fresh mint leaves

60g fetta cheese

40g baby spinach leaves

1 Cook bacon in heated medium frying pan until crisp. Drain on absorbent paper.

2 Combine eggs and water in medium bowl; beat lightly.

3 Heat half the butter in same cleaned pan; add half the egg mixture, sprinkle with half the combined onion, mint and fetta. Cook over medium heat, tilting pan, until egg is just set. Slide omelette from pan, fold in half. Repeat with remaining butter, egg and filling.

4 Serve omelettes with spinach and bacon.
   per serving 49.1g total fat (23.9g saturated fat); 2533kJ (606 cal); 1.8g carbohydrate; 40.5g protein; 1.1g fibre

turkish-style pizza with minted yogurt

preparation time 15 minutes **cooking time** 35 minutes

2 teaspoons olive oil

1 small brown onion (80g), chopped finely

1 clove garlic, crushed

300g lamb mince

pinch cayenne pepper

1 teaspoon ground cumin

½ teaspoon ground cinnamon

1 teaspoon grated lemon rind

1 tablespoon lemon juice

½ cup (125ml) beef stock

1 medium tomato (150g), chopped finely

2 tablespoons roasted pine nuts

2 tablespoons finely chopped fresh mint

430g loaf turkish bread

⅓ cup (95g) yogurt

1 tablespoon finely chopped fresh mint, extra

1 Preheat oven to 220°C/200°C fan-forced.

2 Heat oil in medium frying pan, add onion and garlic; cook, stirring, until onion is soft. Add lamb; cook, stirring, until browned. Add spices; stir until fragrant.

3 Add rind, juice, stock and tomato to pan; cook, stirring, over medium heat until most of the liquid is evaporated. Remove from heat; stir in nuts and mint.

4 Place bread on oven tray; press lamb mixture evenly over top of bread leaving 3cm border.

5 Cover pizza with foil; bake, in oven, 10 minutes. Remove foil; bake further 10 minutes or until browned lightly.

6 Cut bread into thick slices; serve topped with combined yogurt and extra mint.
per serving 34.1g total fat (8.1g saturated fat); 4067kJ (973 cal); 104g carbohydrate; 56.3g protein; 8.5g fibre

LIGHT MEALS

warm potato and smoked chicken salad

preparation time 20 minutes cooking time 15 minutes

300g kipfler potatoes

2 cups (300g) frozen broad beans

250g smoked chicken breasts, sliced thinly

1 small red onion (100g), sliced thinly

50g rocket

1 tablespoon drained baby capers, rinsed

PARSLEY DRESSING

¼ cup firmly packed fresh
flat-leaf parsley leaves

2 tablespoons olive oil

1 tablespoon lemon juice

1 clove garlic, crushed

1 teaspoon dijon mustard

1   Boil or steam potatoes and beans, separately, until tender.

2   Meanwhile, make parsley dressing.

3   Combine remaining ingredients in large bowl.

4   Cut hot potatoes into thin wedges. Peel away grey-coloured outer shells from broad beans. Add potato, beans and dressing to salad; toss gently.

PARSLEY DRESSING Blend or process parsley and oil until finely chopped. Transfer to small bowl; whisk in juice, garlic and mustard.

per serving 27.9g total fat (5.1g saturated fat); 2537kJ (607 cal); 36.1g carbohydrate; 44.1g protein; 16.8g fibre

LIGHT MEALS

19

linguine with garlic and oil

preparation time 15 minutes cooking time 15 minutes

200g linguine

¼ cup (60ml) extra virgin olive oil

2 cloves garlic, chopped finely

1 fresh long red chilli, sliced thinly

¼ cup finely chopped fresh flat-leaf parsley

1 Cook pasta in large saucepan of boiling water until just tender; reserve ¼ cup (60ml) of the cooking liquid. Drain pasta, return to pan.

2 Meanwhile, combine oil, garlic and chilli in medium frying pan; heat gently, stirring, until garlic and chilli are soft and fragrant.

3 Toss pasta with oil mixture, reserved cooking liquid and parsley.
   per serving 28.5g total fat (4.1g saturated fat); 2450kJ (586 cal); 68.6g carbohydrate; 11.6g protein; 4.2g fibre

spiced beef and hummus wrap

preparation time 15 minutes cooking time 10 minutes

2 beef sirloin steaks (440g)

1 tablespoon middle-eastern spice mix

2 pieces mountain bread or lavash

¼ cup (60g) hummus

½ baby cos lettuce

1 large tomato (220g), sliced thickly

2 tablespoons Greek-style yogurt

1 Sprinkle beef with spice mix; cook on heated, oiled grill plate (or grill or barbecue) until cooked as desired. Cover, stand steaks 5 minutes then slice thinly.

2 Top bread with hummus, lettuce, steak, tomato and yogurt; roll up to form wrap.
   per serving 28.2g total fat (11.2g saturated fat); 2822kJ (675 cal); 43.8g carbohydrate; 27.6g protein; 7g fibre

roasted vegetables with eggplant

preparation time 15 minutes **cooking time** 50 minutes

1 small green capsicum (150g)

1 large red capsicum (350g)

1 large yellow capsicum (350g)

1 medium eggplant (300g)

1 clove garlic, unpeeled

200g okra, trimmed

2 tablespoons lemon juice

1 teaspoon tahini

150g mushrooms, sliced thickly

125g cherry tomatoes

6 yellow patty-pan squash (180g), halved

cooking-oil spray

⅓ cup loosely packed fresh basil leaves

½ teaspoon sumac

1 Preheat oven to 220°C/200°C fan-forced. Lightly oil large baking dish.

2 Quarter capsicums; discard seeds and membranes; place, skin-side up, in baking dish. Using fork prick eggplant all over; place in baking dish with garlic. Roast vegetables, uncovered, about 30 minutes or until skins blister. Cover capsicum pieces with plastic or paper for 5 minutes; peel away skin then slice capsicum thickly. Cover to keep warm.

3 Place okra onto oiled oven tray; spray with oil. Place okra into oven with capsicums; roast, uncovered, about 20 minutes or until just tender.

4 When cool enough to handle, peel eggplant and garlic. Coarsely chop eggplants; finely chop garlic. Combine eggplant and garlic in medium bowl with juice and tahini; cover to keep warm.

5 Meanwhile, cook mushroom in lightly oiled small frying pan, stirring, until tender. Add tomatoes and squash; cook, covered, until tomatoes just soften.

6 Combine capsicum, okra and tomato mixture in large bowl with basil; divide between serving plates, top with eggplant mixture. Sprinkle with sumac; serve immediately.

per serving 4.2g total fat (0.3g saturated fat); 961kJ (230 cal);
22.9g carbohydrate; 16.5g protein; 16.4g fibre

fresh salmon and pasta salad

preparation time 10 minutes cooking time 20 minutes

250g salmon fillets

250g farfalle

¾ cup (90g) frozen peas

⅓ cup (80g) sour cream

1 tablespoon lemon juice

1 tablespoon green peppercorns, rinsed, drained

1 tablespoon coarsely chopped fresh dill

2 trimmed celery stalks (200g), sliced thinly

2 tablespoons coarsely chopped fresh chives

1 Cook salmon in heated oiled large frying pan until cooked as desired. Drain on absorbent paper.
2 Meanwhile, cook pasta in large saucepan of boiling water until almost tender; add peas. Cook until pasta is tender; drain.
3 Combine sour cream, juice, peppercorns and dill in small bowl.
4 Place salmon in large bowl; using fork, flake salmon. Add celery, chives, sour cream mixture, pasta and peas to bowl; toss gently.
   per serving 26.4g total fat (12.7g saturated fat); 3344kJ (800 cal); 92.5g carbohydrate; 42.6g protein; 8.6g fibre

chicken caesar salad

preparation time 15 minutes cooking time 10 minutes

1 small baguette (150g)

2 tablespoons olive oil

1 egg yolk

1 clove garlic, quartered

1 tablespoon lemon juice

½ teaspoon dijon mustard

5 drained anchovy fillets

¼ cup (60ml) olive oil

50g parmesan cheese, shaved

½ large cos lettuce, torn

2 cups (200g) coarsely chopped cooked chicken

1 Preheat oven to 180°C/160°C fan-forced.
2 Cut bread into 2cm cubes; combine bread and oil in medium bowl. Place bread on oven tray; cook about 10 minutes or until browned lightly.
3 Blend or process egg yolk, garlic, juice, mustard and half the anchovy until smooth. With motor operating, add oil in a thin, steady stream; process until dressing just thickens.
4 Just before serving, combine cheese, lettuce, chicken, croutons and remaining anchovy in large bowl; toss gently. Drizzle with anchovy dressing to serve.
   per serving 67.4g total fat (15g saturated fat); 4004kJ (958 cal); 41.2g carbohydrate; 45.9g protein; 4.1g fibre

LIGHT MEALS

chicken pho

preparation time 20 minutes cooking time 10 minutes

1 litre (4 cups) chicken stock

2cm piece fresh ginger (10g), grated

1 clove garlic, crushed

2 tablespoons fish sauce

5cm stick fresh lemon grass (10g), chopped finely

½ teaspoon sambal oelek

2 green onions, sliced thinly

50g dried rice noodles

2 cups (200g) shredded cooked chicken

½ cup (40g) bean sprouts

¼ cup firmly packed fresh mint leaves

2 tablespoons finely chopped fresh coriander

1 Combine stock, ginger, garlic, sauce and lemon grass in medium saucepan; bring to a boil. Reduce heat; simmer, covered, 8 minutes. Remove from heat; stir in sambal oelek and onion.

2 Meanwhile, place noodles in medium heatproof bowl, cover with boiling water; stand until just tender, drain.

3 Divide noodles between serving bowls; top with chicken. Ladle soup over chicken; top with sprouts, mint and coriander.
   per serving 9.4g total fat (3g saturated fat); 1120kJ (268 cal); 11.4g carbohydrate; 33.5g protein; 2.1g fibre

LIGHT MEALS

tuna, corn and bean salad with lemon mayonnaise

preparation time 15 minutes

95g can tuna in brine, drained

125g can red kidney beans, rinsed, drained

125g can corn kernels, rinsed, drained

2 trimmed celery stalks (200g), sliced thinly

¼ cup coarsely chopped fresh flat-leaf parsley

50g baby rocket leaves

2 tablespoons mayonnaise

1 tablespoon lemon juice

1 clove garlic, crushed

1 Combine tuna, beans, corn, celery, parsley and rocket in large bowl.

2 Place remaining ingredients in small jug; whisk to combine dressing.

3 Serve salad drizzled with dressing.

per serving 8g total fat (1.2g saturated fat); 978kJ (234 cal); 20.7g carbohydrate; 15.7g protein; 7g fibre

creamy bacon and corn chowder

preparation time 15 minutes **cooking time** 25 minutes

25g butter

1 small brown onion (80g), chopped finely

2 bacon rashers (140g), chopped coarsely

1 tablespoon plain flour

2 cups (500ml) chicken stock

1 cup (250ml) milk

1 corn cob (400g), trimmed

1 medium potato (200g), chopped finely

2 tablespoons chopped fresh chives

1 Heat butter in large saucepan; cook onion and bacon, stirring, until onion softens.

2 Add flour to pan; cook, stirring, about 1 minute. Gradually stir in stock and milk; bring to a boil. Reduce heat; simmer.

3 Cut kernels from corn cobs. Add corn and potatoes to pan; simmer, uncovered, about 15 minutes or until tender.

4 Serve soup sprinkled with chives.

per serving 23.1g total fat (12.5g saturated fat); 2161kJ (517 cal); 49.6g carbohydrate; 23.8g protein; 8.7g fibre

hokkien noodle salad

preparation time 15 minutes cooking time 5 minutes

250g hokkien noodles

2 green onions, sliced thinly

100g snow peas, sliced thinly

1 cup (160g) shredded cooked chicken

100g chinese barbecued pork, sliced thinly

SOY DRESSING

1 tablespoon light soy sauce

2 teaspoons honey

1 clove garlic, crushed

1cm piece fresh ginger (5g), grated

2 teaspoons lemon juice

1 tablespoon olive oil

1 Make soy dressing.

2 Place noodles in large heatproof bowl, cover with boiling water; separate noodles with fork, drain.

3 Combine onions, snow peas, chicken, pork and noodles in large bowl; toss gently. Just before serving, toss through soy dressing.

SOY DRESSING Place ingredients in screw-top jar; shake well.

per serving 22.9g total fat (6g saturated fat); 2298kJ (533 cal); 41.5g carbohydrate; 37.8g protein; 5.3g fibre

VIDEO NIGHTS

thai chicken in lettuce leaf cups

preparation time 20 minutes

4 large iceberg lettuce leaves

2 teaspoons kecap manis

1 teaspoon sesame oil

1 tablespoon lime juice

1 small zucchini (90g), grated coarsely

1 small carrot (70g), grated coarsely

2 green onions, sliced thinly

1 small red capsicum (150g), sliced thinly

2 cups (200g) shredded cooked chicken

2 teaspoons finely chopped fresh mint

2 tablespoons coarsely chopped fresh coriander

1 tablespoon sweet chilli sauce

1 Trim lettuce leaf edges with scissors. Place leaves in large bowl of iced water; refrigerate.

2 Meanwhile, combine kecap manis, oil and juice in medium bowl. Add zucchini, carrot, onion, capsicum, chicken, mint and half the coriander; toss gently.

3 Dry lettuce; divide leaves between serving plates. Top with chicken mixture; drizzle with combined sweet chilli sauce and remaining coriander.
per serving 10g total fat (2.4g saturated fat); 1024kJ (245 cal); 8.2g carbohydrate; 27.8g protein; 4.6g fibre

fetta dip with asparagus, radish and beans

preparation time 15 minutes cooking time 5 minutes

250g Greek-style yogurt

100g fetta cheese, chopped finely

1 tablespoon coarsely chopped fresh mint

1 tablespoon finely chopped fresh oregano

200g asparagus, trimmed

100g baby greens beans, trimmed

4 radishes (140g), trimmed

1 Combine yogurt, cheese and herbs in medium bowl.

2   Add asparagus and beans to frying pan of boiling water; return to a boil, then drain immediately.

3 Place asparagus and beans in bowl of iced water until cold; drain well.

4 Serve dip with asparagus, beans and radish or, if desired, bread and crackers.
   per serving 20.8g total fat (13.4g saturated fat); 1409kJ (337 cal); 15.4g carbohydrate; 20g protein; 3.8g fibre

prosciutto and rocket pizza

preparation time 8 minutes cooking time 20 minutes

335g pizza base

1 cup (260g) bottled tomato pasta sauce

50g provolone cheese, sliced thinly

50g thinly sliced prosciutto

25g baby rocket leaves

1 teaspoon extra virgin olive oil

1 Preheat oven to 220°C/200°C fan-forced.

2 Place pizza base on oven tray; top with sauce, cheese and prosciutto. Bake about 20 minutes or until cheese has melted.

3 Serve pizza topped with rocket and drizzled with oil.
   per serving 18.2g total fat (6.4g saturated fat); 2934kJ (7.2 cal); 101.4g carbohydrate; 28.7g protein; 8.7g fibre

beef burger with garlic mayonnaise and grilled onions

preparation time 15 minutes cooking time 15 minutes

300g beef mince

1 tablespoon tomato sauce

1 tablespoon packaged breadcrumbs

1 tablespoon olive oil

1 medium brown onion (150g), sliced thinly

⅓ cup (100g) whole egg mayonnaise

1 clove garlic, crushed

2 burger buns

40g rocket

100g canned baby beetroot, grated coarsely

1 Combine beef, sauce and breadcrumbs in medium bowl; shape mixture into two patties.

2 Heat half the oil in medium frying pan; cook patties until browned both sides and cooked through. Remove from pan; cover to keep warm.

3 Heat remaining oil in pan, add onion; cook, stirring, until soft.

4 Meanwhile, combine mayonnaise and garlic in small bowl.

5 Preheat grill. Split each roll in half; toast buns until browned lightly. Top rolls with patties, garlic mayonnaise, rocket, beetroot and onion.

per serving 39.7g total fat (8.1g saturated fat); 3536kJ (846 cal); 76.5g carbohydrate; 42.8g protein; 7.1g fibre

caramelised onion, pumpkin and lamb pizza

preparation time 10 minutes cooking time 45 minutes

2 teaspoons olive oil

1 large brown onion (200g), sliced thinly

300g piece pumpkin, sliced thinly

335g pizza base

¼ cup (65g) bottled tomato pasta sauce

125g bocconcini cheese, sliced thinly

200g lamb fillets

25g baby rocket leaves

1 Preheat oven to 240°C/220°C fan-forced.

2 Heat oil in medium saucepan; cook onion, covered, over low heat, stirring occasionally, about 20 minutes or until caramelised.

3 Meanwhile, place pumpkin, in a single layer, on lightly oiled oven tray; roast in oven, uncovered, until just tender.

4 Place pizza base on oven tray; spread with sauce, top with cheese and pumpkin. Cook, uncovered, about 15 minutes or until pumpkin is browned lightly.

5 Meanwhile, cook lamb in lightly oiled medium frying pan over very high heat until cooked as desired. Cover lamb; stand 5 minutes then slice thinly.

6 Serve pizza topped with caramelised onion, lamb and rocket.
per serving 30.1g total fat (12.1g saturated fat); 3841kJ (919 cal); 105.4g carbohydrate; 51.5g protein; 9.8g fibre

fajitas with guacamole and salsa cruda

preparation time 30 minutes cooking time 15 minutes

1 clove garlic, crushed

1 tablespoon lemon juice

1 teaspoon ground cumin

2 teaspoons olive oil

300g lamb strips

1 small red capsicum (150g), sliced thickly

1 small green capsicum (150g), sliced thickly

1 small yellow capsicum (150g), sliced thickly

1 small red onion (100g), sliced thickly

4 large flour tortillas

GUACAMOLE

1 small avocado (200g)

1 tablespoon finely chopped fresh coriander

½ small white onion (40g), chopped finely

2 teaspoons lemon juice

SALSA CRUDA

1 medium tomato (150g), seeded, chopped finely

1 fresh small red thai chilli, chopped finely

¼ cup coarsely chopped fresh coriander

1 clove garlic, crushed

½ small white onion (40g), chopped finely

1 tablespoon lemon juice

1 Combine garlic, juice, cumin and oil in medium bowl; add lamb, stir to coat in mixture. Cover; refrigerate.

2 Meanwhile, make guacamole.

3 Combine ingredients for salsa cruda in small bowl.

4 Cook lamb in heated oiled large frying pan, stirring, until browned all over and cooked as desired. Remove from pan; cover to keep warm.

5 Cook capsicums and onion, in batches, in pan, stirring, until just softened.

6 Meanwhile, heat tortillas according to instructions on packet.

7 Return lamb and capsicum mixture to pan; stir gently over medium heat until heated through. Divide fajita mixture between serving plates; serve with tortillas, guacamole and salsa cruda.

GUACAMOLE Place avocado in small bowl; mash roughly with fork. Add remaining ingredients, stir gently to combine.

per serving 40.6g total fat (11.1g saturated fat); 3382kJ (809 cal);
61.1g carbohydrate; 45.6g protein; 7.9g fibre

TIPS Any firm white fish can be used. Beer can be replaced with soda water, if preferred.

beer-battered fish and chips

preparation time 15 minutes (plus standing time) **cooking time** 20 minutes

500g potatoes

peanut oil, for deep-frying

¾ cup (110g) self-raising flour

½ cup (125ml) beer

½ cup (125ml) cold water

4 skinless flathead fillets (440g)

1 Preheat oven to 160°C/140°C fan-forced.
2 Cut potatoes lengthways into 1cm slices; cut each slice lengthways into 1cm wide pieces. Stand potato pieces in large bowl of cold water 30 minutes. Drain; pat dry with clean tea towel.
3 Heat oil in large saucepan; cook chips, in batches, about 4 minutes or until just tender but not browned. Drain on absorbent paper.
4 Reheat oil; cook chips, in batches, until crisp and golden brown. Drain on absorbent paper; spread out on oven tray; keep warm in oven.
5 Whisk flour, beer and water in small bowl until smooth.
6 Reheat oil. Dip fish in batter; deep-fry until browned, crisp and just cooked through. Drain on absorbent paper.
7 Serve fish immediately with chips, and lemon wedges, if desired.
   per serving 4.4g total fat (1.2g saturated fat); 2512kJ (601 cal); 73g carbohydrate; 58g protein; 6.1g fibre

pork and cheese quesadillas with guacamole

preparation time 30 minutes cooking time 20 minutes

2 teaspoons olive oil

250g pork mince

1 small green capsicum (150g), chopped finely

1 fresh long red chilli, chopped finely

1 clove garlic, crushed

¼ cup coarsely chopped fresh coriander

4 flour tortillas

1 tablespoon olive oil, extra

1 cup (125g) grated cheddar cheese

GUACAMOLE

1 large avocado (320g), chopped coarsely

½ small egg tomato (45g), seeded, chopped finely

½ small red onion (50g), chopped finely

½ fresh long red chilli, chopped finely

2 tablespoons finely chopped fresh coriander

1 tablespoon lime juice

1 Heat oil in medium frying pan; cook pork, stirring, about 10 minutes or until browned. Add capsicum, chilli and garlic; cook, stirring, until fragrant. Remove from heat, stir in coriander.

2 Make guacamole.

3 Brush one side of the tortillas with the extra oil. Turn two tortillas oiled-side down; spread evenly with pork mixture, sprinkle with cheese. Top with remaining tortillas, oiled side up.

4 Cook tortillas, in batches, in heated sandwich press or large frying pan until browned lightly.

5 Cut quesadillas into quarters; serve with guacamole.

GUACAMOLE Place avocado in small bowl; mash roughly with fork. Add remaining ingredients; stir until combined.

per serving 75.5g total fat (25.1g saturated fat); 4627kJ (1107 cal); 52.3g carbohydrate; 52.6g protein; 5.9g fibre

lemon and garlic cutlets
with broad bean, pea and fetta salad

preparation time 30 minutes cooking time 15 minutes

1 tablespoon olive oil

2 teaspoons finely grated lemon rind

1 tablespoon lemon juice

1 clove garlic, crushed

6 french-trimmed lamb cutlets (300g)

⅔ cup (100g) frozen broad beans

⅓ cup (40g) frozen baby peas

100g snow peas, trimmed, sliced thinly

½ cup coarsely chopped fresh basil

75g fetta cheese, crumbled

½ cup (75g) seeded kalamata olives

LEMON DRESSING

1 tablespoon lemon juice

2 tablespoons olive oil

½ teaspoon dijon mustard

1   Combine oil, rind, juice and garlic in medium bowl; add lamb, turn to
    coat in mixture.
2   Boil, steam or microwave beans and baby peas, separately, until just tender;
    drain. Rinse under cold water; drain. Peel away grey-coloured outer shells
    from broad beans; combine beans and baby peas in large bowl.
3   Meanwhile, make lemon dressing.
4   Cook lamb on heated oiled grill plate (or grill or barbecue) until cooked
    as desired.
5   Place snow peas, basil, cheese, olives and half the dressing in bowl with
    beans and peas; toss gently. Serve salad topped with lamb; drizzle with
    remaining dressing. Sprinkle with a little finely grated lemon rind, if desired.
    LEMON DRESSING Place ingredients for lemon dressing in screw-top jar;
    shake well.
    per serving 49.8g total fat (15.6g saturated fat); 2679kJ (413 cal);
    17.5g carbohydrate; 27.9g protein; 7.6g fibre

EVERYDAY DINNERS

creamy pumpkin and sage ravioli

preparation time 15 minutes **cooking time** 25 minutes

1 tablespoon olive oil

8 fresh sage leaves

400g pumpkin, sliced thinly

1 small leek (200g), chopped finely

2 teaspoons shredded fresh sage

2 teaspoons white balsamic condiment

½ cup (125ml) cream

400g fresh or frozen ricotta ravioli

1 Heat half the oil in medium frying pan; fry sage leaves until bright green; remove with slotted spoon or tongs, drain on absorbent paper.

2 Heat remaining oil in pan, add pumpkin; cook, in batches, until browned both sides and just tender. Turn pumpkin carefully to prevent it breaking; cover to keep warm.

3 Add leek to pan; cook, stirring, about 5 minutes or until softened.

4 Add shredded sage, balsamic and cream to pan; bring to a boil. Reduce heat, simmer, uncovered, until sauce has thickened slightly.

5 Meanwhile, cook pasta in large saucepan of boiling water until just tender; drain.

6 Combine pasta with pumpkin and cream mixture; serve topped with fried sage leaves.

per serving 47g total fat (23.6g saturated fat); 2855kJ (714 cal); 42.2g carbohydrate; 20.8g protein; 6.7g fibre

ocean trout with buttered almonds

preparation time 10 minutes cooking time 10 minutes

4 x 100g ocean trout fillets

2 tablespoons plain flour

1 teaspoon olive oil

40g butter

¼ cup (20g) flaked almonds

1 tablespoon lemon juice

1 Toss fish in flour; shake off excess.
2 Heat oil and half the butter in large frying pan; cook fish, uncovered, until browned both sides and cooked as desired. Drain on absorbent paper; cover to keep warm.
3 Heat remaining butter in same cleaned pan; cook almonds, stirring constantly, until browned lightly. Stir in juice; pour almond mixture over fish. Serve with chips, if desired.

per serving 36.7g total fat (13.6g saturated fat); 2278kJ (545 cal); 9.3g carbohydrate; 44g protein; 2.1g fibre

creamy pesto chicken with gnocchi

preparation time 10 minutes cooking time 25 minutes

400g chicken thigh fillets, chopped coarsely

2 teaspoons olive oil

1 clove garlic, crushed

1 shallot (25g), chopped finely

50g fresh shiitake mushrooms, sliced thickly

¼ cup (60ml) dry white wine

1 tablespoon sun-dried tomato pesto

½ cup (125ml) cream

2 tablespoons coarsely chopped fresh basil

300g fresh gnocchi

1 Heat oil in medium frying pan; cook chicken, in batches, until cooked through. Cover to keep warm.
2 Add garlic, shallot and mushroom to pan; cook, stirring, 2 minutes. Stir in wine; simmer, uncovered, until liquid is almost evaporated. Stir in pesto and cream; bring mixture to a boil. Remove from heat; stir in basil.
3 Meanwhile, cook gnocchi, uncovered, in medium saucepan of boiling water until gnocchi are just tender and float to the surface; drain.
4 Divide chicken and gnocchi between plates; drizzle with creamy pesto.

per serving 60.5g total fat (30.2g saturated fat); 3745kJ (896 cal); 31.2g carbohydrate; 51.9g protein; 3.3g fibre

cajun-style blackened fish with green rice

preparation time 15 minutes cooking time 15 minutes

¾ cup (150g) basmati rice

20g butter

½ small green capsicum (75g), chopped finely

1½ cups (375ml) chicken stock

20g butter, melted

1 green onion, chopped finely

1 tablespoon lemon juice

2 x 200g white fish steaks

2 teaspoons cajun spice mix

4 green onions, sliced thinly

¼ cup finely chopped fresh flat-leaf parsley

½ teaspoon cracked black pepper

1 Place rice in sieve; rinse well under cold water, drain.

2 Meanwhile, heat butter in small saucepan; add capsicum; cook, stirring, until softened.

3 Add rice and stock to pan; bring to a boil, stirring occasionally. Cover pan with a tight-fitting lid, reduce heat to as low as possible; cook rice about 12 minutes or until tender.

4 Meanwhile, combine melted butter, chopped onion and juice in small bowl. Brush half the butter mixture over fish; sprinkle with spice mix. Cook fish in small frying pan until blackened both sides and just cooked through.

5 Stir sliced onions, parsley and pepper into rice.

6 Serve fish with rice, remaining butter mixture, and lemon wedges, if desired.
per serving 18.9g total fat (11.5g saturated fat); 2592kJ (620 cal); 63.1g carbohydrate; 47.7g protein; 1.9g fibre

mushroom and rocket risotto

preparation time 10 minutes cooking time 35 minutes

1 cup (250ml) chicken stock

1¾ cups (430ml) water

25g butter

1 tablespoon olive oil

125g button mushrooms, sliced thickly

1 clove garlic, crushed

1 medium brown onion (150g), sliced thinly

1 cup (200g) arborio rice

2 tablespoons coarsely chopped
fresh flat-leaf parsley

⅓ cup (25g) grated parmesan cheese

125g rocket, trimmed

1 Combine stock and the water in medium saucepan; bring to a boil. Reduce heat, simmer.

2 Meanwhile, heat half the butter and half the oil in large saucepan, add mushroom; cook, stirring, until browned lightly. Add garlic; cook, stirring, until fragrant. Remove from pan; cover to keep warm.

3 Heat remaining butter and oil in pan; cook onion, stirring, until soft. Add rice; stir over medium heat until rice is coated in butter mixture. Stir in ½ cup (125ml) of the stock mixture; cook, stirring, over low heat until liquid is absorbed.

4 Continue adding stock mixture, in ½-cup batches, stirring after each addition until liquid is absorbed. The total cooking time should be about 20 minutes or until rice is tender.

5 Stir mushroom mixture, parsley, cheese and rocket into rice mixture. Serve risotto, topped with extra parmesan cheese flakes, if desired.
per serving 25.2g total fat (11g saturated fat); 2771kJ (663 cal); 88.6g carbohydrate; 18.1g protein; 4.8g fibre

chicken and mixed mushroom stir-fry

preparation time 15 minutes cooking time 10 minutes

250g hokkien noodles

2 teaspoons peanut oil

400g chicken breast fillets, sliced thickly

100g button mushrooms, halved

100g flat mushrooms, sliced thickly

100g swiss brown mushrooms, halved

2 green onions, chopped finely

1 tablespoon mild chilli sauce

¼ cup (60ml) oyster sauce

1 Place noodles in large heatproof bowl, cover with boiling water; separate noodles with fork, drain.

2 Heat half the oil in wok; stir-fry chicken, in batches, until browned all over and cooked through.

3 Heat remaining oil in wok; stir-fry mushrooms, in batches, until browned. Return chicken and mushrooms to wok with noodles, onion and sauces; stir-fry until heated through.

per serving 10.6g total fat (2.2g saturated fat); 2149kJ (514 cal); 42.7g carbohydrate; 56.7g protein; 7.7g fibre

paprika-dusted lamb chops with greek salad

preparation time 15 minutes cooking time 10 minutes

4 lamb loin chops (400g)

1 teaspoon sweet paprika

1 tablespoon olive oil

1 small red capsicum (150g), chopped coarsely

1 small green capsicum (150g), chopped coarsely

1 medium tomato (150g), chopped coarsely

100g fetta cheese, diced into 2cm pieces

2 teaspoons lemon juice

2 tablespoons fresh flat-leaf parsley leaves

1 Sprinkle lamb with paprika. Heat half the oil in large frying pan; cook lamb until browned both sides and cooked as desired. Cover; stand 5 minutes.

2 Meanwhile, combine capsicums, tomato, cheese, juice, parsley and remaining oil in medium bowl; toss gently.

3 Divide salad and lamb between serving plates; serve with lemon wedges, if desired.

per serving 41.3g total fat (18.1g saturated fat); 2362kJ (565 cal); 5.6g carbohydrate; 42.5g protein; 2.4g fibre

lamb shanks in five-spice, tamarind and ginger

preparation time 15 minutes **cooking time** 2 hours 10 minutes

1 teaspoon five-spice powder

½ teaspoon dried chilli flakes

½ cinnamon stick

1 star anise

2 tablespoons soy sauce

2 tablespoons lemon juice

1 tablespoon tamarind concentrate

1 tablespoon brown sugar

4cm piece fresh ginger (20g), grated

1 clove garlic, chopped coarsely

¾ cup (180ml) water

4 french-trimmed lamb shanks (1kg)

250g choy sum, chopped into 10cm lengths

100g sugar snap peas, trimmed

1   Preheat oven to 180°C/160°C fan-forced.

2   Dry-fry five-spice, chilli, cinnamon and star anise in small frying pan until fragrant. Combine spices with sauce, juice, tamarind, sugar, ginger, garlic and the water in medium jug.

3   Place lamb, in single layer, in medium shallow baking dish; drizzle with spice mixture. Roast, uncovered, in oven, turning occasionally, about 2 hours or until meat is almost falling off the bone. Remove lamb from dish; cover to keep warm. Skim away excess fat; strain sauce into small saucepan.

4   Meanwhile, boil, steam or microwave choy sum and peas, separately, until tender; drain.

5   Divide vegetables between serving plates; serve with lamb, drizzled with reheated sauce.
per serving 25g total fat (11.3g saturated fat); 2203kJ (527 cal); 13g carbohydrate; 60.1g protein; 3.5g fibre

spicy chicken with rice noodles

preparation time 10 minutes cooking time 15 minutes

400g chicken thigh fillets, chopped coarsely

1 clove garlic, crushed

2 teaspoons finely chopped fresh lemon grass

2 teaspoons teriyaki sauce

2 teaspoons white sugar

½ teaspoon sambal oelek

½ teaspoon ground cumin

½ teaspoon ground coriander

250g fresh wide rice noodles

1 tablespoon sweet chilli sauce

2 teaspoons peanut oil

250g baby buk choy, quartered

1 Combine chicken, garlic, lemon grass, teriyaki sauce, sugar, sambal oelek and spices in medium bowl.

2 Place noodles in medium heatproof bowl, cover with boiling water; separate noodles with fork, drain. Return noodles to bowl; combine with sweet chilli sauce.

3 Meanwhile, heat half the oil in wok; stir-fry chicken mixture, in batches, until chicken is browned all over and cooked through.

4 Heat remaining oil in wok; stir-fry buk choy until just wilted.

5 Serve chicken mixture with buk choy and noodles.
per serving 20.5g total fat (5.3g saturated fat); 2078kJ (497 cal); 35.3g carbohydrate; 41.3g protein; 3g fibre

lamb tikka curry

preparation time 10 minutes cooking time 1 hour 10 minutes

10g butter

1 small brown onion (80g), sliced thinly

400g diced lamb shoulder

¼ cup (75g) tikka curry paste

¾ cup (195g) bottled tomato pasta sauce

¾ cup (180ml) water

¼ cup loosely packed coriander leaves

¼ cup (70g) yogurt

1 Melt butter in medium saucepan; cook onion, stirring, until soft. Add lamb; cook, stirring, 5 minutes or until lamb is browned all over.

2 Stir in curry paste; cook 1 minute. Add sauce and the water; bring to a boil. Reduce heat, simmer, covered, 45 minutes. Simmer, uncovered, a further 10 minutes or until lamb is tender and sauce has thickened slightly.

3 Serve curry with coriander, yogurt, and warmed chapatti, if desired.
per serving 35.5g total fat (13g saturated fat); 2383kJ (570 cal); 15.9g carbohydrate; 44.2g protein; 6.1g fibre

orecchiette with lamb and peas

preparation time 20 minutes cooking time 35 minutes

2 tablespoons olive oil

1 small brown onion (80g), chopped finely

1 clove garlic, crushed

300g lamb mince

1 fresh small red thai chilli, sliced thinly

250g orecchiette pasta

1 cup (120g) frozen peas

1 medium tomato (150g), seeded, chopped finely

GREMOLATA

¼ cup finely chopped fresh flat-leaf parsley

1 clove garlic, crushed

1 teaspoon finely grated lemon rind

1 Make gremolata.

2 Heat half the oil in medium frying pan, add onion and garlic; cook, stirring, until onion is soft. Add lamb and chilli; cook, stirring, until lamb is well browned. Cover to keep warm.

3 Meanwhile, cook pasta in large saucepan of boiling water until just tender. Reserve ¼ cup (60ml) of the cooking liquid; drain pasta.

4 Boil, steam or microwave peas until tender; drain.

5 Toss pasta in large bowl with lamb mixture, peas, reserved cooking liquid, tomato and remaining oil; serve sprinkled with gremolata.
GREMOLATA Combine ingredients in small bowl.
per serving 30.4g total fat (7.5g saturated fat); 3678kJ (880 cal); 94.8g carbohydrate; 50.5g protein; 10.7g fibre

TIP Casarecce is a short, slightly tubular pasta like a twisted scroll.

spring greens and goat cheese pasta

preparation time 10 minutes **cooking time** 20 minutes

1⅓ (200g) frozen broad beans

250g casarecce pasta

1 tablespoon olive oil

1 small zucchini (90g), sliced thinly

1 clove garlic, crushed

½ cup (60g) frozen peas

80g goat cheese, crumbled

¼ cup loosely packed fresh mint leaves

LEMON AND GARLIC CRUMBS

30g butter

1 clove garlic, crushed

½ teaspoon finely grated lemon rind

½ cup (35g) fresh breadcrumbs

1 Place broad beans in large heatproof bowl, cover with boiling water; stand 10 minutes, drain. When cool enough to handle, peel and discard grey outer shell from beans.

2 Meanwhile, cook pasta in large saucepan of boiling water until just tender; drain. Returnm to pan; cover to keep warm.

3 Meanwhile, make lemon and garlic crumbs.

4 Heat oil in large saucepan, add zucchini, garlic and peas; cook, stirring, about 5 minutes or until zucchini is browned lightly. Add broad beans; cook 1 minute.

5 Combine pasta, zucchini mixture, cheese and mint in large bowl; serve topped with lemon and garlic crumbs.
   LEMON AND GARLIC CRUMBS Heat butter in small frying pan; cook garlic, rind and breadcrumbs, stirring, until breadcrumbs are golden and crisp.
   per serving 30.5g total fat (13.9g saturated fat); 3628kJ (868 cal); 110g carbohydrate; 30g protein; 16.6g fibre

red lentil, mushroom and spinach curry

preparation time 15 minutes cooking time 15 minutes

½ cup (100g) red lentils

1 tablespoon vegetable oil

½ teaspoon cumin seeds

1 small brown onion (80g), sliced thinly

1 clove garlic, crushed

2cm piece fresh ginger (10g), grated

1 small green chilli, sliced thinly

100g button mushrooms, halved

¾ cup (180ml) vegetable stock

¼ cup (60ml) water

½ teaspoon garam masala

125g baby spinach leaves

1 Preheat oven to 180°C/160°C fan-forced.
2 Wash lentils well under running water; drain.
3 Heat oil in wok; stir-fry seeds until fragrant. Add onion, garlic, ginger and chilli; stir-fry until onion is soft. Add mushrooms; stir-fry until browned lightly.
4 Add drained lentils, stock and the water; bring to boil. Reduce heat, simmer, uncovered, about 5 minutes or until lentils are tender.
5 Add garam masala and spinach to curry; stir until spinach is wilted.
6 Serve curry with warmed naan and yogurt, if desired.
   per serving 11g total fat (1.5g saturated fat); 1154kJ (276 cal); 23.3g carbohydrate; 17.2g protein; 10.8g fibre

steamed fish with chilli and ginger

preparation time 15 minutes cooking time 10 minutes

1 baby buk choy (150g), quartered

2 snapper cutlets (400g)

5cm piece fresh ginger (25g), cut into matchsticks

2 green onions, cut into 4cm strips

2 tablespoons soy sauce

½ teaspoon sesame oil

1 fresh small red thai chilli, sliced thinly

½ cup loosely packed fresh coriander leaves

1 Place large heatproof plate inside large bamboo steamer; layer with buk choy then fish. Sprinkle fish with ginger and onion; spoon over sauce and oil. Steam fish, covered, over wok of simmering water, about 5 minutes or until just cooked through.

2 Serve fish topped with chilli and coriander.
   per serving 4.6g total fat (1.4g saturated fat); 957kJ (229 cal); 2.4g carbohydrate; 42.8g protein; 1.6g fibre
   TIP Any firm white fish can be used.

baked mustard pork with caramelised apple

preparation time 10 minutes cooking time 25 minutes

1 small red onion (100g),
cut into thin wedges

2 teaspoons olive oil

400g pork fillets, trimmed

2 tablespoons wholegrain mustard

¼ cup (60ml) apple juice

2 tablespoons water

2 tablespoons coarsely chopped
fresh flat-leaf parsley

30g butter

2 large apples (400g), peeled,
cored, sliced thinly

1 tablespoon brown sugar

1 Preheat oven to 240°C/220°C fan-forced.

2 Combine onion and oil in small flameproof baking dish. Brush pork all over with mustard; place on onion in baking dish. Bake, uncovered, about 20 minutes or until cooked as desired. Remove pork from dish, cover; stand 5 minutes.

3 Place dish over heat; add juice and the water, bring to a boil. Reduce heat; simmer, uncovered, about 3 minutes or until sauce thickens slightly. Stir in parsley.

4 Meanwhile, melt butter in large frying pan. Add apple and sugar; cook, stirring occasionally, about 10 minutes or until caramelised.

5 Slice pork thickly; serve with onion sauce and caramelised apple.
   per serving 23.1g total fat (10.4g saturated fat); 2224kJ (532 cal); 32.1g carbohydrate; 47.8g protein; 5.5g fibre

steak with red wine sauce and lyonnaise potatoes

preparation time 15 minutes cooking time 15 minutes

1 tablespoon olive oil

1 medium brown onion (150g), sliced thinly

10g butter

250g baby new potatoes, sliced thickly

2 tablespoons finely chopped flat-leaf parsley

2 x 200g beef scotch fillet steaks

1 clove garlic, crushed

pinch chilli flakes

¼ cup (60ml) red wine

½ cup (125ml) beef stock

100g baby green beans, trimmed

1 Heat half the oil in large frying pan; cook onion, stirring, until soft. Remove from pan. Heat remaining oil and butter in pan; cook potatoes about 10 minutes or until browned and tender. Return onions to pan with parsley; toss gently.

2 Meanwhile, cook beef in lightly oiled large frying pan until cooked as desired; remove from pan, cover to keep warm. Add garlic and chilli to pan; cook until fragrant. Add red wine, bring to a boil. Stir in stock; reduce heat, simmer, uncovered, until sauce is reduced by half. Strain sauce into small jug.

3 Meanwhile, boil, steam or microwave beans until just tender; drain.

4 Serve beef with red wine sauce, potatoes and beans.
per serving 25.7g total fat (9.1g saturated fat); 2261kJ (541 cal); 21.9g carbohydrate; 48.3g protein; 5g fibre

spaghetti with mussels and clams

preparation time 15 minutes cooking time 15 minutes

250g mussels

250g clams

2 tablespoons water

2 tablespoons dry white wine

250g spaghetti

2 tablespoons extra virgin olive oil

1 clove garlic, crushed

1 fresh small red thai chilli, chopped finely

1 medium tomato (150g), seeded, chopped coarsely

¼ cup coarsely chopped fresh flat-leaf parsley

1   Scrub mussels; remove beards. Rinse clams.
2   Combine the water and wine in medium saucepan; bring to a boil. Add mussels and clams; reduce heat, simmer, covered, about 5 minutes or until mussels open (discard any that do not). Strain cooking liquid through fine sieve into medium bowl; reserve ¼ cup (60ml), discard remainder. Strain reserved liquid again, into small jug. Cover mussels and clams to keep warm.
3   Cook pasta in large saucepan of boiling water until just tender; drain.
4   Meanwhile, heat oil in small frying pan; cook garlic and chilli, stirring, until fragrant. Add tomato and reserved cooking liquid; bring to a boil.
5   Place pasta, mussels, clams and tomato mixture into large bowl with parsley; toss gently.
    per serving 20.3g total fat (3g saturated fat); 2805kJ (671 cal); 88.8g carbohydrate; 26.1g protein; 5.6g fibre

SPECIAL DINNERS

provençal-style fish soup with garlic toast

preparation time 15 minutes cooking time 20 minutes

400g can chopped tomatoes

100g char-grilled red capsicum, chopped coarsely

1 tablespoon olive oil

1 clove garlic, crushed

¼ teaspoon fennel seeds

1 cup (250ml) fish stock

1 cup (250ml) water

150g firm white fish fillet, chopped coarsely

150g uncooked peeled prawns

1 tablespoon coarsely chopped fresh dill

GARLIC TOAST

2 thick slices crusty bread

1 clove garlic, halved

1 tablespoon olive oil

1 Blend or process undrained tomatoes with capsicum until smooth.

2 Heat oil, garlic and seeds in medium saucepan over low heat, stirring, about 3 minutes or until fragrant.

3 Add tomato mixture, stock and the water; bring to a boil. Reduce heat, simmer, uncovered, 10 minutes.

4 Meanwhile, make garlic toast.

5 Add fish and prawns to soup; simmer, uncovered, about 3 minutes or until fish is just cooked through.

6 Serve soup sprinkled with chopped fresh dill and accompanied with garlic toast.

GARLIC TOAST Rub bread with garlic, brush with olive oil. Cook in heated grill pan until browned and crisp both sides.

per serving 24.4g total fat (3.3g saturated fat); 2040kJ (488 cal); 27.6g carbohydrate; 37.3g protein; 4.1g fibre

lamb cutlets with salsa verde and parsnip puree

preparation time 15 minutes cooking time 25 minutes

1 large parsnip (350g), chopped coarsely

1 cup (250ml) chicken stock

2 tablespoons cream

6 french-trimmed lamb cutlets (300g)

¼ cup coarsely chopped fresh flat-leaf parsley

¼ cup coarsely chopped fresh basil

¼ cup coarsely chopped fresh mint

1 green onion, sliced thinly

2 tablespoons extra virgin olive oil

1 tablespoon lemon juice

1   Place parsnip and stock in medium saucepan; bring to a boil. Reduce heat, simmer, uncovered, 10 minutes or until parsnip is soft and stock is almost evaporated. Blend or process parsnip until smooth, return to pan; stir in cream, cover to keep warm.

2   Meanwhile, cook lamb on heated oiled grill plate (or grill or barbecue) until cooked as desired.

3   To make salsa verde, combine herbs, onion, oil and juice in small bowl.

4   Serve cutlets with salsa verde and parsnip puree.
    per serving 40.7g total fat (14.5g saturated fat); 2186kJ (523 cal); 17.6g carbohydrate; 20.3g protein; 4.9g fibre

salmon confit with fennel and herbs

preparation time 10 minutes cooking time 20 minutes

2 x 200g salmon fillets

1 clove garlic, sliced thinly

1 cup (250ml) extra virgin olive oil, approximately

1 small fennel bulb (200g), sliced thinly

¼ cup (60ml) dry white wine

2 teaspoons grated lemon rind

1 tablespoon chopped fresh fennel fronds

1 tablespoon chopped fresh chervil

1   Preheat oven to 120°C/100°C fan-forced.

2   Place salmon in small ovenproof dish, just large enough to fit. Sprinkle salmon with garlic; add enough oil to cover salmon completely. Cook salmon, uncovered, about 20 minutes or until cooked as desired. Remove salmon from oil; drain on absorbent paper.

3   Heat 1 tablespoon of the salmon cooking oil in small frying pan; cook fennel, stirring, until softened. Add wine and rind; cook 5 minutes or until wine is reduced by half. Stir in fronds and chervil.

4   Divide fennel mixture between plates, top with salmon. Garnish with extra fresh chervil, if desired.
    per serving 10.8g total fat (1.9g saturated fat); 656kJ (157 cal); 0.7g carbohydrate; 12.5g protein; 0.7g fibre

char-grilled veal with tomato, capers and basil

preparation time 10 minutes **cooking time** 20 minutes

4 baby eggplants (240g), halved lengthways

2 small zucchini (180g), sliced thickly

2 tablespoons extra virgin olive oil

2 x 170g veal cutlets

1 medium egg tomato (75g),
seeded, chopped finely

½ small red onion (50g), chopped finely

1 clove garlic, crushed

1 tablespoon drained baby capers, rinsed

1 tablespoon balsamic vinegar

1 tablespoon fresh baby basil leaves

1 Brush eggplant and zucchini with half the oil; cook, in batches, on heated grill plate (or grill or barbecue) until browned and tender. Transfer to plate; cover to keep warm.

2 Cook veal on heated, oiled grill plate (or grill or barbecue) until browned and cooked as desired. Transfer to plate; cover, stand 10 minutes.

3 Meanwhile, combine tomato, onion, garlic, capers, vinegar and remaining oil in small bowl.

4 Divide eggplant and zucchini between plates; top with cutlets and tomato mixture, sprinkle with basil.

per serving 22.1g total fat (3.5g saturated fat); 1572kJ (376 cal);
7.6g carbohydrate; 33.9g protein; 5.4g fibre

honey dijon lamb racks with potato and kumara gratin

preparation time 40 minutes (plus refrigeration time) cooking time 1 hour

1 tablespoon olive oil

1 teaspoon dijon mustard

2 tablespoons red wine vinegar

1 clove garlic, crushed

1 tablespoon honey

2 x 4 french-trimmed lamb cutlet racks (300g)

1 small kumara (250g)

2 small potatoes (240g)

2 teaspoons plain flour

¾ cup (180ml) cream, warmed

¼ cup (60ml) milk, warmed

⅓ cup (35g) grated pizza cheese

1 Combine oil, mustard, vinegar, garlic and honey in large bowl; add lamb, turn to coat all over in marinade. Cover; refrigerate 3 hours or overnight.

2 Preheat oven to 200°C/180°C fan-forced. Grease deep 1 litre (4-cup) ovenproof dish.

3 Using V-slicer, mandoline or sharp knife, cut kumara and potatoes into 2mm-thick slices; place half the kumara slices, overlapping slightly, in dish. Top with half the potato, overlapping slices slightly. Repeat layering with remaining kumara and potato.

4 Blend flour with a little of the cream in medium jug to form a smooth paste; stir in remaining cream and milk. Pour cream mixture over potato and kumara.

5 Cover gratin with foil; cook about 40 minutes or until vegetables are tender. Uncover gratin; sprinkle with cheese. Cook about 10 minutes or until cheese browns lightly. Stand gratin 5 minutes before serving.

6 Meanwhile, drain lamb; reserve marinade. Place lamb on wire rack in large shallow baking dish; cook, uncovered, in oven for the last 35 minutes of gratin cooking time or until cooked as desired. Cover to keep warm.

7 Bring reserved marinade to a boil in small saucepan. Reduce heat; simmer sauce, uncovered, 5 minutes. Serve gratin with lamb, drizzled with sauce.
per serving 66.2g total fat (36.1g saturated fat); 3795kJ (908 cal); 49.2g carbohydrate; 28.4g protein; 4.3g fibre

ricotta gnocchi in fresh tomato sauce

preparation time 10 minutes cooking time 20 minutes

250g firm ricotta cheese

½ cup (40g) finely grated parmesan cheese

¼ cup (35g) plain flour

1 egg, beaten lightly

2 teaspoons extra virgin olive oil

2 medium tomatoes (300g), chopped coarsely

3 green onions, sliced thinly

1 tablespoon coarsely chopped fresh oregano

1 tablespoon balsamic vinegar

1 tablespoon extra virgin olive oil, extra

¼ cup (20g) shaved parmesan cheese

1 Bring large saucepan of water to a boil.

2 Meanwhile, combine ricotta, grated cheese, flour, egg and oil in large bowl. Drop rounded tablespoons of mixture into boiling water; cook, without stirring, until gnocchi float to the surface. Remove from pan with slotted spoon; drain, cover to keep warm.

3 Combine tomato, onion, oregano and vinegar in medium bowl. Top warm gnocchi with fresh tomato sauce; drizzle with extra oil, top with shaved cheese.

per serving 40.5g total fat (17.9g saturated fat); 2367kJ (566 cal); 17.7g carbohydrate; 31.5g protein; 2.8g fibre

oysters with lime, chives and salmon roe

preparation time 5 minutes

rock salt, for serving

24 oysters on the half shell (600g)

1 tablespoon finely chopped fresh chives

2 tablespoons salmon roe

2 limes, cut into wedges

1 Cover a serving platter with rock salt; top with oysters.
2 Sprinkle oysters with chives and top with salmon roe.
3 Serve with lime wedges.
   per serving 4.5g total fat (1.5g saturated fat); 543kJ (130 cal); 1.5g carbohydrate; 18.7g protein; 1g fibre

fish in prosciutto with capers and garlic mayonnaise

preparation time 15 minutes cooking time 20 minutes

2 x 360g plate-sized whole white fish

2 teaspoons finely grated lemon rind

1 clove garlic, sliced thinly

½ cup coarsely chopped fresh flat-leaf parsley

6 slices thin prosciutto (90g)

1 teaspoon drained capers, chopped

GARLIC MAYONNAISE

2 tablespoons whole egg mayonnaise

1 tablespoon lemon juice

½ clove garlic, crushed

1 Preheat oven to 220°C/200°C fan-forced.
2 Wash cavity of fish under cold water; pat dry with absorbent paper.
3 Combine rind, garlic and parsley in small bowl. Stuff parsley mixture into fish cavities. Wrap three slices of prosciutto around each fish.
4 Place fish on baking-paper-lined oven tray; bake 15 minutes. Sprinkle capers over fish; bake a further 5 minutes or until fish is just cooked through.
5 Meanwhile, make garlic mayonnaise.
6 Serve fish with garlic mayonnaise, and lemon wedges, if desired.
   GARLIC MAYONNAISE Combine ingredients in small bowl.
   per serving 12.9g total fat (3g saturated fat); 1384kJ (331 cal); 4.6g carbohydrate; 47.9g protein; 1.5g fibre

cauliflower soup with cheese and bacon toasts

preparation time 20 minutes cooking time 20 minutes

2 teaspoons olive oil

1 small brown onion (80g), chopped coarsely

1 clove garlic, crushed

1 small potato (120g), chopped finely

300g cauliflower, trimmed, chopped

1½ cups (375ml) chicken stock

1 cup (250ml) water

1 tablespoon coarsely chopped fresh chives

CHEESE AND BACON TOASTS

2 bacon rashers (140g), quartered

½ small baguette

1 teaspoon seeded mustard

50g thinly sliced chedder cheese

1 Heat oil in medium saucepan; cook onion and garlic, stirring, until onion is soft but not coloured.

2 Add potato, cauliflower, stock and the water; bring to a boil. Reduce heat, simmer, covered, about 10 minutes or until vegetables are very soft.

3 Meanwhile, make cheese and bacon toasts.

4 Blend or process cauliflower mixture until smooth. Return soup to pan; stir gently over low heat until heated through.

5 Serve soup sprinkled with chives.

CHEESE AND BACON TOASTS Cook bacon under preheated grill until browned and crisp. Slice bread diagonally into 4 thin slices. Grill bread slices until browned lightly, spread with mustard, top with cheese. Grill until cheese melts; top with bacon. Sprinkle with black pepper, if desired.

per serving 20.6g total fat (8.4g saturated fat); 1806kJ (432 cal); 34.6g carbohydrate; 24.6g protein; 5.7g fibre

smoked salmon with gruyère soufflé

preparation time 15 minutes **cooking time** 30 minutes

2 tablespoons plain flour

¾ cup (180ml) milk

10g butter, chopped

3 eggs, separated

⅔ cup (80g) grated gruyère cheese

50g sliced smoked salmon

1 teaspoon drained baby capers, rinsed

2 teaspoons fresh chervil leaves

1 Preheat oven to 200°C/180°C fan-forced. Grease 1 litre (4-cup) ovenproof soufflé dish. Place dish on oven tray.

2 Place flour in small saucepan; gradually whisk in milk until mixture forms a smooth paste. Cook flour mixture over medium heat, whisking constantly, until mixture boils and thickens. Remove from heat; stir in butter.

3 Whisk egg yolks and cheese into flour mixture. Transfer to large bowl.

4 Beat egg whites in small bowl with electric mixer until soft peaks form. Fold egg whites into cheese mixture, in two batches.

5 Pour mixture into dish. Bake in oven about 25 minutes or until soufflé is well risen and browned.

6 Meanwhile, arrange salmon on serving platter; top with capers and chervil.

7 Serve soufflé, immediately, with salmon.

per serving 28.8g total fat (15.3g saturated fat); 1814kJ (434 cal); 12.9g carbohydrate; 31.4g protein; 0.5g fibre

parsley and bocconcini chicken with watercress salad

preparation time 20 minutes cooking time 10 minutes

2 x 200g chicken breast fillets

100g bocconcini cheese, sliced thickly

1 tablespoon finely chopped
fresh flat-leaf parsley

1 clove garlic, crushed

2 teaspoons extra virgin olive oil

WATERCRESS SALAD

50g trimmed watercress

2 small egg tomatoes (120g), quartered

2 tablespoons seeded black olives

½ small red onion (50g), sliced thinly

1 drained anchovy, chopped finely

1 tablespoon lemon juice

1 tablespoon extra virgin olive oil

1   Slit a pocket in one side of each chicken fillet; divide cheese, parsley and garlic between pockets, secure openings with toothpicks.

2   Heat oil in medium frying pan; cook chicken until cooked as desired.

3   Meanwhile, make watercress salad.

4   Serve chicken with watercress salad.

WATERCRESS SALAD Toss watercress, tomatoes, olives and onion in medium bowl. Whisk anchovy and juice in small bowl; gradually whisk in oil until combined. Add dressing to salad; toss gently.

per serving 26.4g total fat (8.2g saturated fat); 2057kJ (492 cal); 5.8g carbohydrate; 56.3g protein; 2.7g fibre

char-grilled prawns with mango chilli salsa

preparation time 15 minutes cooking time 5 minutes

500g uncooked large prawns

MANGO CHILLI SALSA

2 tablespoons lime juice

1 fresh small red thai chilli, chopped finely

1 tablespoon olive oil

1 teaspoon fish sauce

1 teaspoon grated palm sugar

1 small mango (300g), chopped finely

1 small green mango (300g), sliced thinly

½ small red onion (50g), sliced thinly

¼ cup firmly packed fresh coriander leaves

1   Make mango chilli salsa.
2   Cook prawns in their shells on heated, oiled grill plate (or grill or barbecue) until changed in colour and just cooked through.
3   Serve prawns with mango chilli salsa.
   MANGO CHILLI SALSA Combine juice, chilli, oil, sauce and sugar in medium bowl; stir until sugar is dissolved. Add mangoes, onion and coriander; toss gently.
   per serving 10.4g total fat (1.4g saturated fat); 1417kJ (339 cal); 30.4g carbohydrate; 28.6g protein; 3.7g fibre

fillet steaks with roasted parsnip and beetroot

preparation time 20 minutes cooking time 45 minutes

1 medium parsnip (250g), chopped coarsely

150g baby beetroots

2 tablespoons olive oil

1 clove garlic, crushed

1 teaspoon fresh rosemary leaves

1 cup (100g) cauliflower florets

150g fresh asparagus, chopped coarsely

2 x 125g beef fillet steaks

¼ cup (20g) parmesan cheese flakes

1 Preheat oven to 200°C/180°C fan-forced.

2 Place parsnip and beetroot in small baking dish; toss with half the combined oil, garlic and rosemary. Roast, uncovered, 25 minutes.

3 Place cauliflower and asparagus on oven tray; toss with remaining oil mixture. Roast with the parsnip mixture, 20 minutes or until vegetables are browned and tender. When cool enough to handle, halve the beetroot.

4 Meanwhile, cook beef on heated, oiled grill plate (or grill or barbecue) until browned both sides and cooked as desired. Cover to keep warm.

5 Serve beef with vegetables; sprinkle with cheese.
per serving 29.5g total fat (7.8g saturated fat); 2098kJ (502 cal); 19.6g carbohydrate; 36.7g protein; 7.4g fibre

risotto with seared scallops

preparation time 20 minutes cooking time 35 minutes

2 cups (500ml) fish stock

1 cup (250ml) water

pinch saffron threads

1 tablespoon finely chopped fresh chives

2 tablespoons finely chopped
fresh flat-leaf parsley

2 teaspoons finely grated lemon rind

1 tablespoon extra virgin olive oil

1 small brown onion (80g), chopped finely

1 clove garlic, crushed

1 cup (200g) arborio rice

¼ cup (60ml) dry white wine

20g butter

12 scallops, roe removed (300g)

1 Combine stock, the water and saffron in medium saucepan; bring to a boil. Reduce heat, simmer.
2 Combine chives, parsley and rind in small bowl.
3 Heat half the oil in large saucepan; cook onion and garlic, stirring, until onion softens.
4 Add rice to pan; stir about 1 minute or until rice is well coated. Add wine; bring to a boil. Reduce heat, simmer, uncovered, until most of the liquid is evaporated.
5 Stir in ½ cup (125ml) of the stock mixture; cook, stirring, over medium heat until liquid is absorbed. Continue adding stock mixture, in ½-cup batches, stirring after each addition until liquid is absorbed. Cooking time should be about 30 minutes or until rice is just tender. Stir in butter.
6 Heat remaining oil in medium frying pan; cook scallops about 1 minute each side or until browned.
7 Top risotto with scallops, sprinkle with herb mixture; drizzle with extra olive oil, if desired.
per serving 19.1g total fat (7.2g saturated fat); 2579kJ (617 cal); 83.8g carbohydrate; 21.1g protein; 2g fibre

TIP Leftover cakes can be stored in an airtight container in the refrigerator for up to one week. Reheat in microwave oven on HIGH (100%) for 30 seconds before serving.

little lime syrup cakes

preparation time 10 minutes cooking time 25 minutes makes 6

125g butter, chopped

½ cup (110g) caster sugar

2 teaspoons grated lime rind

2 eggs

1 cup (150g) self-raising flour

½ cup (125ml) buttermilk

LIME SYRUP

⅓ cup (80ml) lime juice

½ cup (110g) caster sugar

2 tablespoons water

1 teaspoon grated lime rind

1 Preheat oven to 180°C/160°C fan-forced. Grease 6-hole mini fluted tube pan or texas (¾-cup/180ml) muffin pan.

2 Beat butter, sugar and rind in small bowl with electric mixer until light and fluffy. Add eggs, one at a time, beating until just combined between additions.

3 Transfer mixture to medium bowl; stir in sifted flour and buttermilk.

4 Divide mixture among pan holes, smooth tops. Bake about 25 minutes.

5 Meanwhile, make lime syrup.

6 Stand cakes 5 minutes before turning onto wire rack over a tray. Pour hot lime syrup evenly over hot cakes. Serve cakes warm or cooled with whipped cream, if desired.

LIME SYRUP Combine all ingredients except rind in small saucepan; stir over low heat until sugar dissolves. Bring to a boil; remove from heat. Strain into medium heatproof jug. Stir in rind.

per cake 19.6g total fat (12.1g saturated fat); 1547kJ (370 cal); 43.1g carbohydrate; 5.8g protein; 1g fibre

DESSERTS

steamed chocolate puddings with coffee anglaise

preparation time 20 minutes **cooking time** 25 minutes

60g butter, softened

⅓ cup (75g) caster sugar

1 egg

2 tablespoons finely chopped
stale breadcrumbs

⅓ cup (50g) self-raising flour

1 tablespoon cocoa powder

1 tablespoon milk

2 tablespoons finely chopped
dark eating chocolate

COFFEE ANGLAISE

¾ cup (180ml) milk

1 tablespoon caster sugar

2 egg yolks

2 teaspoons plain flour

2 teaspoons instant coffee granules

1 tablespoon boiling water

1 Grease two ¾-cup (180ml) ovenproof dishes.
2 Beat butter, sugar and egg in small bowl with an electric mixer until
   just combined; stir in breadcrumbs, sifted flour and cocoa, milk and
   chocolate. Spoon into dishes. Top with a piece of baking paper and
   foil, secure with rubber bands or string.
3 Place dishes in deep small frying pan; add enough boiling water to
   come halfway up the sides of dishes. Cover pan with tight-fitting lid;
   boil about 25 minutes or until cooked when tested with a skewer.
   Remove puddings from pan; stand 5 minutes.
4 Meanwhile, make coffee anglaise.
5 Dust puddings with extra sifted cocoa, if desired, and serve with
   coffee anglaise.
   COFFEE ANGLAISE Place milk in small saucepan; bring to a boil.
   Whisk sugar and egg yolks in medium bowl until creamy; add flour
   then slowly whisk in hot milk. Return mixture to pan. Stir over low
   heat, without boiling, until anglaise is thickened slightly. Dissolve
   coffee in the boiling water; stir into anglaise.
   per serving 41.9 total fat (25.3g saturated fat); 3227kJ (772 cal);
   85.6g carbohydrate; 15.5g protein; 2.4g fibre

pecan and chocolate brownies

preparation time 15 minutes cooking time 25 minutes makes 4

40g butter, chopped

100g dark eating chocolate, chopped coarsely

⅓ cup (75g) firmly packed brown sugar

1 egg, beaten lightly

⅓ cup (50g) plain flour

2 teaspoons cocoa powder

25g dark eating chocolate, chopped coarsely, extra

2 tablespoons coarsely chopped pecans

1 Preheat oven to 200°C/180°C fan-forced. Grease four holes of a 6-hole (⅓-cup/80ml) muffin pan.

2 Combine butter, chocolate and sugar in small heavy-based saucepan; stir over low heat until smooth.

3 Transfer mixture to large bowl; stir in egg, sifted flour and cocoa then extra chocolate. Divide mixture among pan holes. Sprinkle with nuts; bake, in oven, about 20 minutes. Stand muffins in pan 5 minutes before turning onto wire rack to cool.
   per muffin 22.9g total fat (14.8g saturated fat); 1685kJ (403 cal); 44.5g carbohydrate; 5g protein; 2.4g fibre

plum tarts

preparation time 10 minutes cooking time 15 minutes

½ sheet ready-rolled puff pastry

1 egg yolk

1 tablespoon milk

4 small ripe plums (300g), sliced thinly

2 teaspoons caster sugar

½ teaspoon ground cinnamon

1 Preheat oven to 220°C/200°C fan-forced. Line oven tray with baking paper.

2 Cut pastry sheet in half, place each half on tray; brush with combined egg yolk and milk.

3 Overlap plum slices on pastry squares, leaving 2cm border. Sprinkle plums with combined sugar and cinnamon.

4 Bake about 15 minutes or until pastry is browned and crisp.
   per serving 12.4g total fat (6.1g saturated fat); 1058kJ (253 cal); 28.4g carbohydrate; 4.7g protein; 3.1g fibre

apricot almond crumbles

preparation time 15 minutes cooking time 30 minutes

400g can apricot halves in natural juice

2 teaspoons brandy

¼ cup (35g) self-raising flour

½ teaspoon ground ginger

2 tablespoons ground almonds

2 tablespoons brown sugar

1 tablespoon caster sugar

50g butter, chopped

1 Preheat oven to 180°C/160°C fan-forced.

2 Drain apricots over small jug; reserve ¼ cup (60ml) juice.

3 Slice apricots and divide between two ¾-cup (180ml) ovenproof dishes; place dishes on oven tray. Combine brandy with reserved juice; pour over apricots.

4 Sift flour and ginger into medium bowl; stir in almonds and sugars, then rub in butter with fingertips.

5 Sprinkle crumble mixture over apricots; bake about 30 minutes or until browned lightly. Serve hot, with ice-cream or cream, if desired.
   per serving 26.2g total fat (13.9g saturated fat); 1869kJ (447 cal); 44.6g carbohydrate; 5.1g protein; 4g fibre

coffee and pecan puddings with caramel sauce

preparation time 15 minutes cooking time 40 minutes

¼ cup (30g) coarsely chopped roasted pecans

⅓ cup (80ml) cream

½ cup (110g) firmly packed brown sugar

30g cold butter, chopped coarsely

50g butter, softened

2 tablespoons caster sugar

1 egg

⅓ cup (50g) self-raising flour

1 tablespoon plain flour

1 tablespoon milk

1 teaspoon finely ground espresso coffee

1 Preheat oven to 180°C/160°C fan-forced. Grease two ¾-cup (180ml) ovenproof dishes.

2 Divide nuts between dishes; place on oven tray.

3 Stir cream, brown sugar and chopped butter in small saucepan over heat, without boiling, until sugar dissolves. Reduce heat; simmer, uncovered, without stirring, about 5 minutes or until mixture thickens slightly. Spoon 2 tablespoons of the sauce over nuts in each dish; reserve remaining sauce.

4 Beat softened butter and caster sugar in small bowl with electric mixer until light and fluffy; beat in egg. Stir in sifted flours, milk and coffee; divide mixture between dishes. Bake, in oven, about 30 minutes. Stand puddings 5 minutes before turning onto serving plates.

5 Reheat reserved sauce; spoon sauce over puddings to serve.
per serving 64.3g total fat (34.8g saturated fat); 4080kJ (976 cal); 94.4g carbohydrate; 9.3g protein; 2.4g fibre

raspberry vanilla ice-cream sandwiches

preparation time 10 minutes

125g strawberries, sliced thickly

2 teaspoons caster sugar

2 scoops raspberry sorbet

6 Lattice biscuits

2 scoops vanilla ice-cream

100g raspberries

1   Combine strawberries and sugar in small bowl.
2   Sandwich sorbet between two biscuits on each serving plate, top with ice-cream and remaining biscuits.
3   Add raspberries to strawberry mixture.
4   Serve ice-cream sandwiches with berry mixture.
    per serving 13.9g total fat (10.3g saturated fat); 1852kJ (443 cal); 71.5g carbohydrate; 7.4g protein; 4.9g fibre

minted fruit salad

preparation time 20 minutes **cooking time** 15 minutes (plus refrigeration time)

¾ cup (180ml) water

2 teaspoons grated palm sugar

1 star anise

1 tablespoon lime juice

½ small pineapple (450g), chopped coarsely

½ small honeydew melon (650g), chopped coarsely

200g fresh lychees, seeded

100g seedless red grapes

¼ cup loosely packed fresh mint leaves, torn

1   Stir the water, sugar and star anise in small saucepan over heat until sugar dissolves. Simmer, uncovered, 10 minutes. Stir in juice. Cover; refrigerate 1 hour. Strain syrup into medium jug; discard star anise.
2   Combine fruit, mint and syrup in large bowl.
    per serving 1g total fat (0g saturated fat); 957kJ (229 cal); 47.3g carbohydrate; 4.5g protein; 6.6g fibre

baked caramel custard with roasted pears

preparation time 10 minutes cooking time 1 hour 5 minutes

¼ cup (55g) caster sugar

1 tablespoon water

½ cup (125ml) cream

¼ cup (60ml) milk

1 egg

1 egg yolk

2 baby brown pears (200g)

15g butter, chopped

1 tablespoon caster sugar, extra

1 Preheat oven to 160°/140°C fan-forced.

2 Place sugar and the water in small saucepan; stir over low heat, without boiling, until sugar is dissolved. Bring to a boil; boil, uncovered, without stirring, until a golden caramel colour.

3 Remove from heat; gradually whisk in cream and milk. Return to heat to melt any undissolved caramel.

4 Beat egg and egg yolk in small bowl with whisk until combined; gradually whisk in cream mixture. Strain custard into medium jug.

5 Place two ½-cup (125ml) ovenproof dishes in medium baking dish. Pour custard into dishes. Pour enough boiling water into baking dish to come halfway up the sides of dishes. Bake, in oven, about 35 minutes or until custard is just set.

6 Remove custards from baking dish; increase oven temperature to 220°C/200°C fan-forced.

7 Slice unpeeled pears lengthways. Place on medium greased oven tray. Dot with butter; sprinkle with half the extra sugar. Bake 15 minutes; turn pears over, sprinkle with remaining sugar, bake a further 15 minutes or until pears are browned and tender.

8 Serve caramel custards with roasted pears.
per serving 39.9g total fat (24.4g saturated fat); 2454kJ (587 cal); 52.7g carbohydrate; 7.4g protein; 1.8g fibre

TIP Without an electric ice-cream maker, freeze mixture until partially frozen; chop coarsely then beat with an electric mixer until smooth. Fold in chopped mango; freeze until firm. Store frozen yogurt in freezer for up to 3 months.

mango frozen yogurt

preparation time 25 minutes **cooking time** 10 minutes (plus refrigeration and freezing time) **makes** 1.5 litres (6 cups)

3 egg yolks

⅔ cup (150g) caster sugar

300ml cream

1¼ cups (310ml) milk

1¾ cups (500g) Greek-style yogurt

2 small ripe mangoes (600g), peeled, chopped coarsely

1   Whisk egg yolks and sugar in medium bowl until light and fluffy.

2   Bring cream and milk almost to a boil in medium saucepan. Remove from heat. Whisking constantly, gradually pour cream mixture into egg mixture.

3   Return custard mixture to pan; cook over low heat, stirring constantly, until mixture thickens and coats the back of a spoon. Do not boil.

4   Transfer mixture to a large bowl; cover, refrigerate until cold.

5   Stir yogurt into cold custard. Churn mixture in an ice-cream maker, following manufacturer's instructions, until beginning to thicken. Add mangoes, churn until firm.

6   Transfer mixture to 1.5-litre (6-cup) freezer-proof container. Cover; freeze about 4 hours or until firm.

7   Serve scooped in glasses with extra sliced mango, if desired.
per serving 32.4g total fat (20.3g saturated fat); 2115kJ (506 cal); 45.4g carbohydrate; 9.6g protein; 1.1g fibre

BASIL an aromatic herb; there are many types, but the most commonly used is sweet basil.

BEETROOT also known as red beets.

BREADS

baguette a French bread that's been formed into a long, narrow cylindrical loaf up to a metre in length. It is also known as a french stick or french loaf.

chapatti a type of Indian bread made from flour, water and salt. Rolled into discs, it is cooked in a very hot pan then steamed until it puffs up like a balloon.

ciabatta in Italian, the word means slipper, the traditional shape of this crisp-crusted, open-textured white sourdough bread.

lavash flat, unleavened bread originating in the Mediterranean; good used as a wrapper or torn and used for dips.

mountain a thin, dry, soft-textured bread. Available from supermarkets and health food stores.

naan thick, leavened bread associated with the tandoori dishes of northern India where it is baked pressed against the inside wall of a heated tandoor (clay oven).

pitta also known as lebanese bread; wheat-flour pocket bread sold in large, flat pieces that separate into two thin rounds. Smaller *pocket pitta* is also available.

tortilla thin, round unleavened bread originating in Mexico; two kinds are available: one made from wheat flour and the other from corn.

turkish also known as pide; comes in long flat loaves as well as individual rounds.

BUK CHOY also known as bok choy, pak choi, chinese white cabbage or chinese chard; has a fresh, mild mustard taste. *Baby buk choy*, also known as pak kat farang or shanghai bok choy, is much smaller and more tender than buk choy.

BUTTER use salted or unsalted (sweet) butter; 125g is equal to one stick of butter.

CAJUN SEASONING a blend of assorted herbs and spices that can include paprika, basil, onion, fennel, thyme, cayenne and tarragon.

CAPSICUM also known as bell pepper or pepper. Discard seeds and membranes before use.

CAYENNE PEPPER *see chilli.*

CELERIAC tuberous root with knobbly brown skin, white flesh and a celery-like flavour.

CHEESE

bocconcini from the diminutive of "boccone", meaning mouthful in Italian; walnut-sized, baby mozzarella, a delicate, semi-soft, white cheese traditionally made from buffalo milk. Sold fresh, it spoils rapidly so will only keep, refrigerated in brine, for 2 days at the most.

fetta a crumbly textured goat- or sheep-milk cheese having a sharp, salty taste.

goat made from goat milk, has a strong, earthy taste. Available in soft, crumbly and firm textures, in various shapes and sizes, and sometimes rolled in ash or herbs.

gruyère a hard-rind Swiss cheese with small holes and a nutty, slightly salty, flavour.

haloumi a firm, cream-coloured sheep-milk cheese matured in brine; somewhat like a minty, salty fetta in flavour. Haloumi can be grilled or fried, briefly, without breaking down. It should be eaten while still warm as it becomes tough and rubbery on cooling.

parmesan also known as parmigiano; is a hard, grainy cow-milk cheese that originated in the Parma region of Italy. The curd for this cheese is salted in brine for a month before being aged for up to 2 years.

pecorino the generic name for cheeses made from sheep milk; if you can't find it, use parmesan.

pizza a commercial blend of varying proportions of processed grated mozzarella, cheddar and parmesan.

provolone a mild stretched-curd cheese; similar to mozzarella when young, becoming hard, spicy and grainy the longer it's aged. Golden yellow in colour with a waxy rind.

ricotta a soft, sweet, moist, white, cow-milk cheese with a low-fat content and a slightly grainy texture. Manufactured from whey (a by-product of other cheese making).

cheddar a semi-hard cow-milk cheese. It ranges in colour from white to pale yellow, and has a slightly crumbly texture.

vintage cheddar cow-milk cheese; ranges in colour from white to pale yellow and has a smooth, fairly hard texture. A long maturing process gives it a strong lingering flavour.

CHILLI available in many different types and sizes. Use rubber gloves when seeding and chopping fresh chillies as they can burn your skin. Removing seeds and membranes lessens the heat level.

cayenne also known as cayenne pepper; a thin-fleshed, long, extremely hot, dried red chilli, usually purchased ground.

dried flakes deep-red, dehydrated chilli slices and whole seeds; good for use in cooking or as a condiment for sprinkling over cooked foods.

red thai also known as "scuds"; tiny, very hot and bright red in colour.

CHINESE BARBECUED PORK also called char siew. Traditionally cooked in special ovens, this pork has a sweet-sticky coating made from soy sauce, sherry, five-spice powder and hoisin sauce. Available from Asian food stores.

CHINESE COOKING WINE also known as hao hsing or chinese rice wine; made from fermented rice, wheat, sugar and salt with a 13.5 per cent alcohol content. Found in Asian food shops; if you can't find it, replace with mirin or sherry.

CHIVES related to the onion and leek; has a subtle onion flavour.

CHOY SUM also known as pakaukeo or flowering cabbage; a member of the buk choy family. Has long stems, light green leaves and yellow flowers, all of which are edible.

CLAMS bivalve mollusc also known as vongole; we use a small ridge-shelled variety.

CORELLA PEARS miniature dessert pear up to 10cm long.

CORIANDER also known as cilantro, pak chee or chinese parsley; bright-green-leafed herb having both pungent aroma and taste. Both the stems and roots are used in Thai cooking: wash well before chopping. Coriander seeds are dried and sold either whole or ground; these must never be used to replace fresh coriander, or vice versa, as the tastes are completely different.

CUMIN also known as zeera or comino; the dried seed of a plant related to the parsley family having a spicy, almost curry-like, flavour.

GLOSSARY

EGGPLANT also known as aubergine.
baby also known as finger or japanese eggplant; very small and slender.

EGGS exercise caution if any recipes in this book call for raw or barely cooked eggs, particularly if there is a salmonella problem in your local area.

FENNEL also known as finocchio or anise; also sometimes the name given to the dried seeds of the plant, which have a stronger licorice flavour.

FIVE-SPICE POWDER a fragrant mixture of ground cinnamon, cloves, star anise, sichuan pepper and fennel seeds. Also known as chinese five-spice.

GARAM MASALA blended spices based on varying proportions of cardamom, cloves, cinnamon, coriander, fennel and cumin, roasted and ground together. Black pepper and chilli can be added for a hotter version.

GINGER
fresh also known as green or root ginger; the thick gnarled root of a tropical plant.
ground also known as powdered ginger; used as a flavouring in cakes, pies and puddings, but cannot be substituted for fresh ginger.

HUMMUS a Middle Eastern salad or dip made from softened dried chickpeas, garlic, lemon juice and tahini (sesame seed paste).

KAFFIR LIME LEAVES also known as bai magrood; looks like two glossy dark green leaves joined end to end, forming a rounded hourglass shape. The dried leaves are less potent so double the number if using them as a substitute for fresh; a strip of fresh lime peel may be substituted for each kaffir lime leaf.

KECAP MANIS *see sauces.*

KUMARA Polynesian name of an orange-fleshed sweet potato often confused with yam.

LATTICE BISCUITS a delicate pastry biscuit, perfect for desserts. The dough is gently rolled into very fine sheets, just like puff pastry, and the biscuits are glazed with a sprinkle of sugar before being baked.

LEMON GRASS a tall, clumping, lemon-smelling and tasting, sharp-edged aromatic tropical grass; the white lower part of the stem is used.

LYCHEES a small fruit from China with a hard shell and sweet, juicy flesh. The white flesh has a gelatinous texture and musky, perfumed taste. Discard the rough skin and seed before using.

MAPLE SYRUP distilled from the sap of maple trees. Maple-flavoured syrup or pancake syrup is not an adequate substitute.

MIDDLE-EASTERN SPICE MIX available from most Middle-Eastern food stores and spice shops; a Moroccan spice blend can be substituted.

MINCE also known as ground meat.

MUSHROOMS
portobello mature swiss browns.
shiitake when fresh are also known as chinese black, forest or golden oak; are large and meaty. When dried, are known as donko or dried chinese mushrooms; rehydrate before use.
swiss brown also known as cremini or roman mushrooms; light brown mushrooms having a full-bodied flavour. Button or cup mushrooms can be substituted.

NOODLES
dried rice also known as rice stick noodles. Made from rice flour and water; available flat and wide or very thin (vermicelli). Must be soaked in boiling water to soften.
hokkien also known as stir-fry noodles; fresh wheat noodles resembling thick, yellow-brown spaghetti needing no pre-cooking before use.
fresh rice also known as ho fun, khao pun, sen yau, pho or kway tiau. Can be purchased in strands of various widths or large sheets weighing about 500g, which are cut into the desired noodle size. Chewy and pure white, they do not need pre-cooking before use.

PALM SUGAR also known as nam tan pip, jaggery, jawa or gula melaka; made from the sap of the sugar palm tree. Light brown to black in colour and usually sold in rock-hard cakes; substitute with brown sugar, if you want.

PARSLEY, FLAT-LEAF also known as continental or italian parsley.

PASTA
casarecce shaped like a narrow twisted and rolled tube; typically made into 5cm lengths.
farfalle bow-tie shaped short pasta; also known as butterfly pasta.
linguine known as flat spaghetti or little tongues because of its shape.
orecchiette small disc-shaped pasta, translates literally as "little ears".
ravioli small, square pasta pockets stuffed with meat, cheese or vegetables.
spaghetti long, thin solid strands of pasta.

PINE NUTS also known as pignoli.

POTATOES
kipfler small, finger-shaped potato with a nutty flavour; great baked and in salads.
sebago oval-shaped, white-skinned potato.

ROCKET also known as arugula, rugula and rucola; a peppery green leaf.

baby rocket leaves are smaller and less peppery than mature rocket.

ROLLED OATS flattened oat grain rolled into flakes and traditionally used for porridge. Instant oats are also available, but use traditional oats for baking.

SAMBAL OELEK (also spelled ulek or olek) Indonesian in origin; a salty paste made from ground chillies and vinegar.

SAUCES
fish also called naam pla or nuoc naam; made from pulverised salted fermented fish (most often anchovies); has a pungent smell and strong taste. Available in varying degrees of intensity, so use according to your taste.
kecap manis a dark, thick, sweet soy sauce. The sweetness is derived from the addition of molasses or palm sugar when brewed.
mild chilli a blend of mild chillies, vinegar, sugar, and other flavourings. Some varieties are also tomato-based.
oyster a rich, brown sauce made from oysters and their brine, cooked with salt and soy sauce, and thickened with starches.
soy also known as sieu; made from fermented soybeans. Several variations are available in supermarkets and Asian food stores; we use Japanese soy sauce unless indicated otherwise.
sweet chilli comparatively mild, fairly sticky and runny bottled sauce made from red chillies, sugar, garlic and white wine vinegar; mostly used as a condiment.
teriyaki Japanese in origin; made from soy sauce, mirin, sugar, ginger and other spices.

STAR ANISE a dried star-shaped pod whose seeds have an astringent aniseed flavour.

TAMARIND CONCENTRATE (or paste) the commercial result of the distillation of tamarind juice into a condensed, compacted paste.

TIKKA CURRY PASTE a medium/mild paste consisting of chilli, coriander, cumin, lentil flour, garlic, ginger, oil, turmeric, fennel, pepper, cloves, cinnamon and cardamom.

VINEGAR BALSAMIC originally from Modena, Italy, there are now many balsamic vinegars on the market ranging in pungency and quality depending on how, and for how long, they have been aged. Quality can be determined up to a point by price; use the most expensive sparingly.

WHITE BALSAMIC CONDIMENT a lighter version of balsamic vinegar; fresh and sweet with a clean taste, it is processed and refined in order to keep it clear and bright.

ZUCCHINI also known as courgette..

MEASURES

One Australian metric measuring cup holds approximately 250ml; one Australian metric tablespoon holds 20ml; one Australian metric teaspoon holds 5ml.

The difference between one country's measuring cups and another's is within a two- or three-teaspoon variance, and will not affect your cooking results. North America, New Zealand and the United Kingdom use a 15ml tablespoon.

All cup and spoon measurements are level. The most accurate way of measuring dry ingredients is to weigh them. When measuring liquids, use a clear glass or plastic jug with the metric markings.

We use large eggs with an average weight of 60g.

DRY MEASURES

METRIC	IMPERIAL
15g	½oz
30g	1oz
60g	2oz
90g	3oz
125g	4oz (¼lb)
155g	5oz
185g	6oz
220g	7oz
250g	8oz (½lb)
280g	9oz
315g	10oz
345g	11oz
375g	12oz (¾lb)
410g	13oz
440g	14oz
470g	15oz
500g	16oz (1lb)
750g	24oz (1½lb)
1kg	32oz (2lb)

LIQUID MEASURES

METRIC	IMPERIAL
30ml	1 fluid oz
60ml	2 fluid oz
100ml	3 fluid oz
125ml	4 fluid oz
150ml	5 fluid oz (¼ pint/1 gill)
190ml	6 fluid oz
250ml	8 fluid oz
300ml	10 fluid oz (½ pint)
500ml	16 fluid oz
600ml	20 fluid oz (1 pint)
1000ml (1 litre)	1¾ pints

LENGTH MEASURES

METRIC	IMPERIAL
3mm	⅛in
6mm	¼in
1cm	½in
2cm	¾in
2.5cm	1in
5cm	2in
6cm	2½in
8cm	3in
10cm	4in
13cm	5in
15cm	6in
18cm	7in
20cm	8in
23cm	9in
25cm	10in
28cm	11in
30cm	12in (1ft)

OVEN TEMPERATURES

These oven temperatures are only a guide for conventional ovens.
For fan-forced ovens, check the manufacturer's manual.

	°C (CELSIUS)	°F (FAHRENHEIT)	GAS MARK
Very slow	120	250	½
Slow	150	275-300	1-2
Moderately slow	160	325	3
Moderate	180	350-375	4-5
Moderately hot	200	400	6
Hot	220	425-450	7-8
Very hot	240	475	9

CONVERSION CHART

INDEX

118

ARE YOU MISSING SOME OF THE WORLD'S FAVOURITE COOKBOOKS?

The Australian Women's Weekly Cookbooks are available from bookshops, cookshops, supermarkets and other stores all over the world. You can also buy direct from the publisher, using the order form below.

To order: Mail or fax – photocopy or complete the order form above, and send your credit card details or cheque payable to: Australian Consolidated Press (UK), ACP Books, 10 Scirocco Close, Moulton Park Office Village, Northampton NN3 6AP
phone (+44) (0)1604 642 200
fax (+44) (0)1604 642 300
email books@acpuk.com
or order online at www.acpuk.com
Non-UK residents: We accept the credit cards listed on the coupon, or cheques, drafts or International Money Orders payable in sterling and drawn on a UK bank. Credit card charges are at the exchange rate current at the time of payment.
Postage and packing UK: Add £1.00 per order plus £1.75 per book.
Postage and packing overseas: Add £2.00 per order plus £3.50 per book.
All pricing current at time of going to press and subject to change/availability.
Offer ends 31.12.2008

TITLE	RRP	QTY	TITLE	RRP	QTY
100 Fast Fillets	£6.99		Indian Cooking Class	£6.99	
After Work Fast	£6.99		Japanese Cooking Class	£6.99	
Beginners Cooking Class	£6.99		Just For One	£6.99	
Beginners Thai	£6.99		Just For Two	£6.99	
Best Food Desserts	£6.99		Kids' Birthday Cakes	£6.99	
Best Food Fast	£6.99		Kids Cooking	£6.99	
Breads & Muffins	£6.99		Kids' Cooking Step-by-Step	£6.99	
Cafe Classics	£6.99		Low-carb, Low-fat	£6.99	
Cakes Bakes & Desserts	£6.99		Low-fat Feasts	£6.99	
Cakes Biscuits & Slices	£6.99		Low-fat Food for Life	£6.99	
Cakes Cooking Class	£6.99		Low-fat Meals in Minutes	£6.99	
Caribbean Cooking	£6.99		Main Course Salads	£6.99	
Casseroles	£6.99		Mexican	£6.99	
Casseroles & Slow-Cooked Classics	£6.99		Middle Eastern Cooking Class	£6.99	
Cheap Eats	£6.99		Mince in Minutes	£6.99	
Cheesecakes: baked and chilled	£6.99		Moroccan & the Foods of North Africa	£6.99	
Chicken	£6.99		Muffins, Scones & Breads	£6.99	
Chicken Meals in Minutes	£6.99		New Casseroles	£6.99	
Chinese & the foods of Thailand, Vietnam, Malaysia & Japan	£6.99		New Curries	£6.99	
Chinese Cooking Class	£6.99		New Finger Food	£6.99	
			New French Food	£6.99	
Christmas Cooking	£6.99		New Salads	£6.99	
Chocolate	£6.99		Party Food and Drink	£6.99	
Chocs & Treats	£6.99		Pasta Meals in Minutes	£6.99	
Cocktails	£6.99		Potatoes	£6.99	
Cookies & Biscuits	£6.99		Rice & Risotto	£6.99	
Cupcakes & Fairycakes	£6.99		Salads: Simple, Fast & Fresh	£6.99	
Detox	£6.99		Sauces Salsas & Dressings	£6.99	
Dinner Lamb	£6.99		Sensational Stir-Fries	£6.99	
Dinner Seafood	£6.99		Simple Healthy Meals	£6.99	
Easy Curry	£6.99		Soup	£6.99	
Easy Midweek Meals	£6.99		Stir-fry	£6.99	
Easy Spanish-Style	£6.99		Superfoods for Exam Success	£6.99	
Essential Soup	£6.99		Sweet Old-Fashioned Favourites	£6.99	
Food for Fit and Healthy Kids	£6.99		Tapas Mezze Antipasto & other bites	£6.99	
Foods of the Mediterranean	£6.99		Thai Cooking Class	£6.99	
Foods That Fight Back	£6.99		Traditional Italian	£6.99	
Fresh Food Fast	£6.99		Vegetarian Meals in Minutes	£6.99	
Fresh Food for Babies & Toddlers	£6.99		Vegie Food	£6.99	
Good Food for Babies & Toddlers	£6.99		Wicked Sweet Indulgences	£6.99	
Greek Cooking Class	£6.99		Wok Meals in Minutes	£6.99	
Grills	£6.99				
Healthy Heart Cookbook	£6.99		TOTAL COST:	£	

Mr/Mrs/Ms _____

Address _____

_____ Postcode _____

Day time phone _____ email* (optional) _____

I enclose my cheque/money order for £ _____

or please charge £ _____

to my: ☐ Access   ☐ Mastercard   ☐ Visa   ☐ Diners Club

Card number ⸢ | | | | | | | | | | | | | | | ⸣

Expiry date _____ 3 digit security code *(found on reverse of card)* _____

Cardholder's name_____ Signature _____

* By including your email address, you consent to receipt of any email regarding this magazine, and other emails which inform you of ACP's other publications, products, services and events, and to promote third party goods and services you may be interested in.

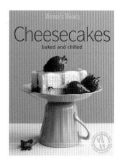

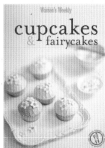

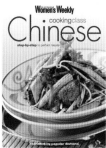
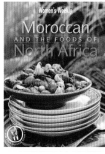

You'll find these books and more available on sale at bookshops, cookshops, selected supermarkets or direct from the publisher (see order form page 119).

TEST KITCHEN
Food director Pamela Clark
Food editor Cathie Lonnie
Photographers Alan Benson, Steve Brown, Ben Dearnley, Joe Filshie, Chris Jones, Andre Martin, Philip Le Masurier, Louise Lister, Prue Ruscoe, Robert Reichenfeld, George Seper, Brett Stevens
Stylists Wendy Berecry, Janelle Bloom, Julz Beresford, Marie-Helene Clauzon, Yael Grinham, Jane Hann, Mary Harris, Amber Keller, Jessica Sly, Sarah O'Brien, Stephanie Souvlis

ACP BOOKS
Editorial director Susan Tomnay
Creative director & designer Hieu Chi Nguyen
Senior editor Wendy Bryant

Director of sales Brian Cearnes
Marketing manager Bridget Cody
Business analyst Ashley Davies

Chief executive officer Ian Law
Group publisher Pat Ingram
General manager Christine Whiston
Editorial director (WW) Deborah Thomas

RIGHTS ENQUIRIES
Laura Bamford, Director ACP Books
lbamford@acpuk.com

Produced by ACP Books, Sydney.
Printed by Dai Nippon, c/o Samhwa Printing Co Ltd, 237-10 Kuro-Dong, Kuro-Ku, Seoul, Korea.
Published by ACP Books, a division of ACP Magazines Ltd, 54 Park St, Sydney; GPO Box 4088, Sydney, NSW 2001.
Ph: (02) 9282 8618 Fax: (02) 9267 9438.
acpbooks@acpmagazines.com.au
www.acpbooks.com.au

To order books, phone 136 116 (within Australia).
Send recipe enquiries to:
recipeenquiries@acpmagazines.com.au

Australia Distributed by Network Services, phone +61 2 9282 8777 fax +61 2 9264 3278 networkweb@networkservicescompany.com.au
United Kingdom Distributed by Australian Consolidated Press (UK), phone (01604) 642 200 fax (01604) 642 300 books@acpuk.com
New Zealand Distributed by Netlink Distribution Company, phone (9) 366 9966 ask@ndc.co.nz
South Africa Distributed by PSD Promotions, phone (27 11) 392 6065/7 fax (27 11) 392 6079/80 orders@psdprom.co.za

The Australian Women's Weekly: Just for two Includes index.
ISBN 978 1 86396 677 1
1. Cookery for two. I. Clark, Pamela.
II. Title: Australian Women's Weekly.
641.5612
© ACP Magazines Ltd 2007
ABN 18 053 273 546